Wake Up, Mummy

WITHDRAWN

D0581471

WITHDRAWN

Wake Up, Mummy

*The heartbreaking true story of an
abused little girl whose mother was
too drunk to notice*

ANNA LOWE

EBURY
PRESS

1 3 5 7 9 10 8 6 4 2

First published in 2011 by Ebury Press, an imprint of Ebury Publishing
A Random House Group company

Copyright © Anna Lowe and Jane Smith 2011

Anna Lowe and Jane Smith have asserted their right to be identified
as the authors of this Work in accordance with the Copyright,
Designs and Patents Act 1988

All rights reserved. No part of this publication may be reproduced,
stored in a retrieval system, or transmitted in any form or by any means,
electronic, mechanical, photocopying, recording or otherwise, without
the prior permission of the copyright owner

The Random House Group Limited Reg. No. 954009

Addresses for companies within the Random House Group can be
found at www.randomhouse.co.uk

A CIP catalogue record for this book is available from the British Library

The Random House Group Limited supports The Forest Stewardship
Council (FSC), the leading international forest certification organisation.
All our titles that are printed on Greenpeace approved FSC certified
paper carry the FSC logo. Our paper procurement policy can be
found at www.rbooks.co.uk/environment

Mixed Sources
Product group from well-managed
forests and other controlled sources
www.fsc.org   Cert no. TT-COC-2139
© 1996 Forest Stewardship Council

Printed in the UK by CPI Cox & Wyman, Reading, RG1 8EX

ISBN 9780091940515

To buy books by your favourite authors and register for offers visit
www.rbooks.co.uk

Contents

Author's note   vii

Prologue   1

1   Cause and effect   6

2   Unfit parents   19

3   A new beginning   31

4   This is my daddy   52

5   Carl: the end of the new beginning   68

6   Beaten, abused and unloved   84

7   Bad becomes worse   107

8   Worse becomes wretched   124

9   Trying – and failing   142

10   As one door opens, another one shuts   166

11   Losing hope   189

12   Accepting the inevitable   204

13   Guilt, remorse and unfounded optimism   226

14   Desperate for love   244

15   The decision that changed my life   259

16   Bereaved, betrayed and determined   278

17   Fighting back   297

Epilogue   310

Author's note

THE EVENTS DESCRIBED in the first chapter of this book took place before I was born and when I was just a baby, so what I've written about them is based on what I've been told by other people. I've included them because I think they help to explain some of the reasons why my mother was the way she was.

Many people had effects on my life when I was growing up, most of them negative. But one of the most significant influences of all was the abuse – mental, physical and sexual – that was inflicted on me by my mother's boyfriend, Carl.

I didn't understand what Carl was doing to me at the time, and it wasn't until some years later that I realised he'd taken my virginity one morning when I was just six years old. I'd woken up with terrible earache and my mother had left me with Carl while she went out to get me some medicine. And it was then – as I lay in the bed beside him, crying with pain – that he did something to me that was quite different from the horrible, disgusting things he'd done so many times before.

Saying that my mother 'went out to get me some medicine' makes her sound like a considerably better parent than she actually was. In reality, though, she probably caused me more hurt and more long-lasting psychological damage than anyone else in my miserably unhappy childhood.

There were reasons why my mother failed so dismally in her duty to protect and care for me and my brother when we were children, and I suppose I understand – at least partly – why she behaved in the way she did. But when someone recently called me 'an amazingly forgiving woman', it made me wonder if I have, in fact, truly forgiven my mother.

For years, almost every aspect of my behaviour was influenced by anger and bitterness. I was resentful about what happened to me when I was a child and, above all, about the things my mother's love of alcohol and lack of maternal care had deprived me of – including my childhood, a normal family life and any chance of being happy.

Living with my mother was like living in a nightmare in which the only certainty was that nothing good ever lasted. So I doubt whether I'd have been able – or willing – to start building a relationship with her as an adult if she hadn't turned out to be a much better grandmother to my children than she had ever been a mother to me.

Perhaps 'tenacious' and 'stubborn' are better words to describe me than 'forgiving', because I think these are the characteristics that have been of most help to me on the many occasions when I've had to struggle to survive. And if I had to think of something positive that came out of my life as a child, it would be that I know how essential it is for children to have the love and stability that were so lacking in my own childhood.

My mother's parents and some of my aunts and uncles showed me, briefly, that there is a better way to live, and I have a great deal to thank them for. I'm grateful, too, to my brother, for being there when I needed someone as a child, and for making me feel – then and now – that I'm not entirely alone.

For me, though, the most important driving force of all is the absolute love I have for my children.

Prologue

I HATED BATH time. The prospect of it hung like a black cloud over almost every single day. As soon as I got home from school, I'd start to dread it. I'd glance repeatedly at the clock in the kitchen or the one on the ugly mantelpiece in the living room and wish that the hands would stop turning and the minutes would stop ticking away so that bath time never came. However, I think it would have taken an earthquake, at least, to make Carl miss it. It didn't matter how much I prayed, the time always came when he bellowed at my brother and me, 'Bath!'

Normally, I tried not to be in the same room as Carl when bath time came around, because I always clung to the hope that if he couldn't actually see me, one day he might forget. But he never did.

On this particular day, Carl, my mother and I had been watching something on television and I was sitting on the dirty floor at the side of the sofa, clutching my knees to my chest, when Carl shouted the word. Instantly, my stomach tied itself into a tight, hard knot and a sour-tasting liquid rushed into my mouth so that I had to keep swallowing to stop myself being sick.

I hated Carl and I was very frightened of him, but I was determined not to jump to my feet immediately and scurry off up the stairs like a scared little rabbit. Instead, I sat completely still, pretending to be engrossed in the adverts that had followed the television programme, despite the fact that my eyes no longer seemed to be able to focus on the screen.

Suddenly, Carl leaned forward, grabbed my ear lobe between his thumb and forefinger and squeezed it painfully, digging his yellow fingernails into the tender flesh and jerking my head to the side as he bellowed into my face, 'Oi! Did you hear what I just said? Looks like those ears of yours are going to need a good scrubbing out in the bath tonight.' Then he kicked me hard on my leg with the toe of his boot and shouted, 'I said, it's bath time.'

I twisted my head away from him, tugging my throbbing ear lobe out of his grasp, and scrambled to my feet. I knew without looking at him the expression that would be on his ugly, unshaven face – the triumph in his nasty, spiteful, piggy eyes and the self-satisfied smirk on his thin lips.

I glanced towards my mother, but she continued to stare at the television screen, showing no sign that she'd seen or heard any part of what had just happened, until she reached out her hand to touch Carl's arm and said, 'You're too good to that kid. How many other men would leave a comfy seat on the sofa to give their stepdaughter a bath? She doesn't deserve you.'

'I'm not his stepdaughter! He's not my stepdad!' I yelled at my mother.

But she was right about one thing, although not in the way she meant it: I didn't deserve Carl's attention. At just six years old, what had I ever done to deserve Carl's relentless, brutal abuse?

By the time I reached the top of the stairs, my little brother, Chris, was already in the bathroom. I could see him through the open doorway, standing, shivering, beside the bath in his T-shirt and underpants, his scrawny little shoulders hunched in miserable resignation.

Carl had followed me up the stairs, and when he'd run water into the bath – not scalding this time, which was at least something to be grateful for – he told us to strip off and get in.

Chris climbed in first, feeling the water with his toes for a moment before sitting down with his back to the taps. Then I got in and sat facing him and Carl stepped into the water behind me, pushing me forward roughly with his foot to make space for his repulsive, naked, tattooed body.

I hated it when Carl sat behind me – I hated him being in the bath anyway, but my heart always beat louder and faster when I couldn't see what he was doing.

My brother was shaking like a frightened dog waiting for the next vicious, unprovoked kick from its master and I smiled at him – a small, quick smile – and then nodded my head once to try to reassure him. Or perhaps I was trying to reassure myself.

At that moment, Carl almost lifted me out of the water from behind and I felt a sharp, burning pain, as though someone had tried to push a red-hot poker inside me. I screamed, twisting my body as I tried to wriggle free of Carl's grip. And Chris cried out too, responding instinctively to the shocked fear in my voice, and then he leaped to his feet and jumped out of the bath like a tightly coiled spring being suddenly released.

Immediately, I shot forward into the space where Chris had been sitting and spun round to look at Carl, who was cupping his hands between his legs as if he was trying to hide something, and looking nervously towards the bathroom door. In the split-second that his attention was distracted, I seized my opportunity and followed my brother out of the bath and across the landing into our bedroom.

Carl shouted after us, but we were already tugging on our nightclothes over wet skin. Then we ran down the stairs to where our mother was still watching television and drinking rum in the relative safety of the living room.

Carl got his revenge, though, as he always did, because that night he beat us with his belt for dripping water on the bathroom floor. And the next night he made sure that he held me more tightly when he climbed into the bath behind me.

1
Cause and effect

BERNADETTE RESTED HER head against the spindles of the high-backed oak chair and looked down at the baby that was sucking with single-minded determination at her breast. She ran her finger along the downy softness of her daughter's cheek and then turned her head towards the open door. It was early spring, but the day had all the sun-soaked languor of midsummer and Bernadette released a slow sigh of contentment as she listened to the sound of the children playing in the garden.

As a child herself, she had sat on the same wooden chair on more occasions than she could have counted, her feet dangling nearer the ground with each year that passed. She closed her eyes and imagined herself aged seven or eight years old, swinging her legs and half-listening to the pleasantly lilting voices of her mother and aunt as they drank tea from flower-patterned china cups and discussed the family issues of the day. It felt good to be back once more in the familiar security of her aunt's kitchen.

'We're going to call her Judith.' Bernadette stroked the baby's cheek again as she spoke.

'It's a good name.' Her Aunt Martha paused for a moment and smiled at her, before turning to lift the heavy, cast-iron kettle from the range cooker and pour water into a large, brown teapot that stood warming beside it.

A shadow fell across the baby's head and Bernadette looked again towards the open back door.

'Sarah? Is that you?' she asked, raising a hand to shield her eyes against the brightness of the sunlight that framed the dark silhouette of a child standing in the doorway. 'Come into the kitchen, darling, so that I can see your face.'

The child didn't move, and as Bernadette's eyes grew accustomed to the sharply contrasted light and darkness, she saw that her niece was holding something in her arms.

'He won't say anything,' Sarah whispered. 'He was lying on his tummy…in the stream.'

As if in confirmation of her words, large drops of water splashed on to the step at her feet.

With a gasp of sudden understanding, Bernadette sprang from the chair, startling the baby as she almost tore its mouth from her breast. But Martha had already crossed the flagstone floor and was snatching Stephen from Sarah's grasp. Sweeping one hand across the kitchen table, she sent plates and cups crashing to the floor as she gently laid the child on the hard, scrubbed-pine surface.

Bernadette thrust the howling baby into Sarah's still-outstretched arms and ran to her son's side. Her face bore an expressionless mask of apparent incomprehension as she watched Martha put her ear to Stephen's mouth and then feel his neck with her fingertips, searching for a pulse.

A sound more animal than human rose from somewhere deep inside Bernadette. But Martha barely heard it, as she placed the heels of her hands on the little boy's fragile chest and pressed firmly. She counted aloud, 'One, two, three,' and then bent down, putting her mouth over Stephen's and blowing her own life-giving breath into his limp and unresponsive body.

Bernadette clasped her son's hand and began to whisper, 'Please, God. Please, God. Please, God.'

The other children had followed Sarah in from the garden and they were clustered around her, their eyes wide with fear, when Martha suddenly stood upright, her face flushed with anxiety and exertion, and looked towards them.

'Becky!' Martha's tone was sharp and commanding. 'Stop your crying now, Becky. Stephen needs your help. Run down the road to Mrs Ryan and tell her to fetch the doctor. Quick now! Go as fast as you can.'

Becky released a single sob as she fled down the pathway that wound around the house to the front garden, and the woman turned back towards the table. Once again, Martha placed her large, capable hands on Stephen's chest, while Bernadette continued to whisper her prayer and tried in vain to block out the voice in her head that kept repeating with cruel insistency, *It's too late. It's too late.*

Even before they heard the sound of the doctor's car in the lane, Bernadette knew that the voice in her head was right: God was not going to save her child.

On a warm, sunny, early-spring morning, three-year-old Stephen was pronounced dead where he lay on the kitchen table, and Bernadette thought her heart would break.

BURYING THEIR SON was the hardest thing Bernadette and her husband Charlie had ever had to do. But not only had she lost her precious child, it seemed also as though his death had severed the bond between Bernadette and her baby daughter. Of course, she knew it wasn't the baby's fault that she'd been feeding her in the kitchen of her aunt's house instead of being outside, watching her two young sons and their cousins play by the shallow stream that ran through the bottom of the garden. She knew, too, that it was neither reasonable nor rational to blame Judith for having absorbed her attention that day. But she simply couldn't help herself.

Over the next few years, Bernadette and her husband had three more children and loved them all. But the fact remained that every time she looked at Judith, she thought of Stephen, and every time she thought of Stephen she felt an ache in her heart so profoundly painful that sometimes, for just one guilty, fleeting moment, she wished the two children could have exchanged places.

THE YEARS PASSED and Judith grew from restless toddler to difficult child to angry, aggressive teenager. As her siblings became strong in mind and body, she developed into a manipulative, argumentative, sneaky and vindictive liar who demanded attention, threw spectacular tantrums when she didn't get her own way, and indulged in mood swings that were as uncontrollable as they were frightening.

Judith's well-behaved, well-adjusted brothers and sisters all grew up to be – or to marry – successful professional people, and became the sort of adults their parents could be proud of. It was just Judith who was different. By turns depressive and wildly unpredictable, she was a constant source of embarrassment to everyone connected with her. By the time she was 13, she was playing truant from school, spending her days stealing to fund what quickly became a serious drinking problem, and indulging in a promiscuity that was shocking even for the relatively liberal-minded 1960s.

However, although Judith's behaviour was extreme by any standards, she somehow managed to continue to function convincingly enough for Bernadette to refuse to consider the possibility that her daughter was in a state of mental crisis.

An accomplished and determined deceiver, Judith caused trouble wherever she went. Her irrational, self-destructive, supremely self-centred behaviour resulted in repeated and often very distressing conflicts, confrontations and misunderstandings between her parents and siblings. Inevitably, she gained a reputation for being an attention-seeking troublemaker who was best avoided.

Today, someone would probably have picked up on the fact that she was suffering from a mental illness. In those days, however, there was such stigma attached to mental health problems that they were rarely discussed, and therefore most people knew little about them. So it's unlikely that Judith's parents suspected there was anything seriously wrong with their daughter, and that she was ill rather than 'bad'.

Bernadette was proud, respectable and respected, a pillar of her local church community and a good woman who had suffered a terrible tragedy in the loss of her beloved son. Appearances and conformity mattered to her, though, and she would rather have died than lay herself open to the humiliation of being judged by her friends and neighbours. She and her husband based their parenting on sound Christian principles. They were strict with their children, but had close, loving relationships with them – all of them, that is, except Judith. It was Judith alone who caused problems in the family, and although Bernadette tried to love her, Judith constantly pushed her mother away, frightening her with her irrational and explosive behaviour and creating chaos and unhappiness all around her.

As a teenager, Judith resented what she saw as her parents' total lack of understanding and sympathy for her. Whenever they *did* try to help her, though, she flew into a rage, hurling foul abuse at them and accusing them of interfering in her life. No amount of cajoling or pleading seemed to have any effect.

And, throughout all those years, Bernadette was haunted by crushing guilt for her son's death, and by the fear that Judith might be able to sense her struggle to love her. Sometimes, when Judith was out with her unsuitable and mostly unpleasant friends, Bernadette would wrestle with the conflict of worrying about what trouble her daughter might be getting into and gratitude for the few hours of peace and harmony that were restored in the house whenever she wasn't at home. It was a deeply unchristian, un-maternal thought and it filled Bernadette with remorse and shame. But she simply couldn't help thinking it.

Then, one day, driven to the end of her tether by her daughter's snarling aggression, Bernadette walked silently into the hallway, lifted her coat from the stand by the front door, picked up her handbag and left the house. She *had* to talk to someone. She had never hated anyone in her life, but sometimes, when she looked at her daughter…

A tear slid down the side of her nose and she wiped it away impatiently with the back of her hand. She hadn't wanted anyone, ever, to know what went on behind the front door of her home. But Judith was single-handedly ripping the family apart, and something had to be done to try to stop her, for all their sakes. As Bernadette walked down the street with feigned brisk purpose, she decided she would talk to her priest. If only she could make Judith learn to have faith in God, she was certain her daughter would be able to turn her life around.

The priest at Bernadette's local church was also a family friend and a regular visitor to the house. So he already knew a little of the trouble and distress that had been caused over the years by Judith's reckless selfishness. Even so, he was shocked to see the strain and exhaustion so clearly evident on Bernadette's face, and he agreed readily to speak to Judith.

Now all Bernadette had to do was find a way to persuade her daughter to meet with the priest.

For once, though, it seemed that God heard one of Bernadette's prayers and Judith responded to her mother's nervous request by grunting something incomprehensible, shrugging her shoulders and muttering, 'I s'pose.'

Judith's family were often convinced that she hated and despised them. In reality, however, she felt as though her life was spiralling out of control. She was always quick to excuse her erratic, destructive and promiscuous behaviour and to blame everyone but herself for anything that went wrong. And she was loud in defence of her right to do whatever she pleased. But underneath the tough hostility of her facade was a child who was frightened by the power of her own emotions and who often thought she was losing her mind.

A few days after her mother's visit to the priest, Judith slammed the front door behind her and set off from the house to walk the short distance to the rectory. Twenty minutes later, she was sitting in an ancient, overstuffed leather armchair in a room lined by equally overstuffed bookshelves, letting the words spill out of her.

The priest sat with his hands resting on the desk in front of him, his fingertips lightly touching, while

Judith talked about her fears, the chaos of her uncontrollable emotions, and how she often did things she was ashamed of simply because she didn't know how *not* to do them.

No one knows what the priest said to Judith that day. Clearly, though, when he offered to give her a lift home in his car, she felt comfortable enough to agree. Bernadette heard the sound of its engine idling for a moment on the road outside the house and then, a few seconds later, Judith burst through the front door, flung her bag on the hall table and exploded into the kitchen, shouting, 'That fucking bastard! Thanks, Mum, for delivering me into the hands of that lecherous old pervert.'

Bernadette's heart began to thump. She longed to cover her ears with her hands and block out the sound of her daughter's terrible accusations. Instead, she turned away, clutched the edge of the kitchen sink so tightly her fingers ached, and prayed, 'Please, God, when I turn around, *please* let her be gone.'

But Judith was determined to be heard.

'Shall I tell you what he's really like, that saintly old man you admire so much?' Her voice had risen to a scream. 'I told him stuff I've never told anyone before, and do you know what he did? That fucking bastard brought me home in his car and tried to put his hand up my skirt. Thanks, Mum! You've really helped a lot.'

Breathless with fury, Judith glared at her mother's trembling back. And then, suddenly, Bernadette spun round, took a step towards her daughter and slapped her hard across the face.

'How dare you!' Bernadette shouted, anger erupting from her violently shaking body. 'How dare you tell your filthy, evil lies about that good man? Stop it, Judith! For pity's sake, stop lying. Stop trying to make yourself important and special. Don't you realise that trouble and hurt follow you wherever you go? Stop it – now – or I don't know what's going to become of you.'

For a moment, Judith stood completely still, gently touching the red mark on her cheek with her fingertips, her eyes flashing with resentment and hurt. Then she burst into tears and ran from the room.

No one ever really knew whether Judith's story about the priest was true. It certainly became more elaborate and outrageous each time she told it, and she always blamed him for her lifelong distrust of the Church in general. Otherwise, it changed nothing in her life. She continued to be vicious, both verbally and physically, and to alienate anyone who might have been able to help her.

Sometimes, Judith's heavy drinking was an attempt at self-medication. When she was manic, alcohol would slow the racing of her mind; and when she was depressed, it would mask her intense sadness and feelings of hopelessness – for a while, at least. But it was also simply an addiction, too, and she would do almost anything to raise the money to buy drink.

At the age of 14, she returned to school drunk one day after lunch, hit one of her teachers and was expelled. After that, no other school in the area would take her, and her parents eventually enrolled her at a college, which at least allowed her to continue with some sort of education and gave a degree of structure to her days. Unfortunately, however, it also meant that she was mixing with older teenagers and had much more freedom than she'd had at school, and she began to drink even more determinedly, going to pubs at lunchtimes and in the evenings – which is where she met Paul.

Paul and Judith were brought together by their mutual love of alcohol – apart from which, they seem to have had little in common. Paul was a couple of years older, a short, stocky, violent and vicious bully with an almost palpable air of aggression and a deeply rooted, immutable hatred and distrust of women. He clearly wasn't the sort of young man Judith's parents would have approved of – which may well have been part of his appeal for her.

When she was just 16 years old, Judith became pregnant – whether as a deliberate act of defiance or as the result of a drunken accident, no one knows. If it *was* intended as a means of giving one more twist to the knife she'd embedded in her mother's heart many years previously, it had the desired effect. As deeply religious people, her parents were mortified by the thought of what their priest (and neighbours) would say if it became known that their teenage daughter was about to become an unmarried mother. So, although they disliked Paul, they insisted the couple should marry.

In fact, Judith's father also had another reason for wishing his daughter to be married before her child was born: having been abandoned by his own mother as a small boy, his experiences had left him with the unshakeable opinion that children need two parents.

Three months after the wedding, I was born – the daughter of a mentally ill, alcoholic, teenage mother who could barely take care of herself, and a violent, misogynistic, drunken and abusive father.

I didn't stand a chance.

2

Unfit parents

MY MOTHER WAS a horrible teenager and a dangerously indifferent, self-absorbed parent. Perhaps her behaviour was due to having grown up feeling unloved – or, at least, less loved than her siblings. Or perhaps she'd absorbed some of her own mother's guilt and felt as though she was somehow responsible for the death of the brother she never knew. Or maybe it was all entirely due to her mental illness and alcoholism. I'll never know. But, despite all the terrible things that happened to me over the next few years, the consequences of which I'll have to live with for the rest of my life, and despite all the misery my mother caused, I've always loved her. I think I've always known she couldn't really help herself. So although I can't actually forgive her for opening the door and pushing me into the lion's den when I was six years old, I do know that, sober and in her right mind, she wouldn't have wanted me to suffer in the way I did.

My father, on the other hand, seems to have had no 'medical' excuse that I'm aware of for his cruel treatment of his mother, my mother and me. He may have had traumas in his own childhood. I know how that feels. But I know also that although some of the things that happen to you as a child may leave deep scars which never really heal, you still have a choice about how you behave towards other people. And he chose to treat his own daughter with cruel contempt.

My father wasn't present during my birth – I don't think most men were, in those days. He arrived at the hospital when it was all over, glanced into my cot, hissed at my mother, 'You can both fuck off,' and left. He'd wanted a son, and he saw no reason to hide his disgust at being presented with a worthless daughter. He felt that he'd been forced into marriage by his wife's parents, coerced into shouldering responsibilities he'd normally have avoided, and he was bitterly resentful.

He returned to the hospital a couple of days later to take me and my mother home. Then he went to the registry office, where he registered only the first of the two names my mother had chosen for me. And that, he felt, was all he was required to do. While I was a baby, he totally avoided having any contact with me – he never held me, fed me or changed my nappy – and he never spoke to me other than with anger and dislike.

My mother's father worked in construction, doing contracts that took him all over the world, and after I was born he found jobs for himself and my father in the Middle East. So, when I was one month old, my parents, my grandparents and I left England and went to live there for a year.

Some years later, on one of the many occasions when my father was shouting about how useless I was and how he cursed the day I'd been born, he told me he'd tried to sell me to a man he'd met in the Middle East when I was baby. Apparently, the man had admired my blonde hair and blue eyes and wanted to 'buy' me as a wife for his son when I reached the age of 12. My father could hardly believe his luck. He agreed to an immediate down-payment and then a second, larger, sum of money when the man came to England to 'collect' me 11 years later. The man explained to my father that once he'd accepted the initial payment, there would be no going back on the deal, and that, wherever we were living when the time came, he *would* find us. My father just laughed and assured him he wouldn't change his mind. His discovery that he could sell his 'worthless' daughter was the silver lining to what had previously seemed a very dark cloud, and he certainly wasn't going to let the opportunity slip from his grasp.

Luckily for me, though, my grandfather found out about the plan before any money could change hands, and he put a stop to it.

When the building contract came to an end, we all returned to England, my father joined the army and my parents and I went to live in a house on a military base. Our new home was some miles away from where my grandparents lived, and it may have been because they were no longer there to see what was happening to my mother that my father's violence towards her escalated – and continued to do so even after she gave birth to the son he'd always wanted. She became little more than a punch bag, subjected to a constant barrage of physical and verbal abuse. And every time he viciously assaulted her, she lost a little more of her spirit.

My mother was still just a teenager, barely able to look after herself. So it was pretty much a foregone conclusion that she wasn't very good at caring for two young children, particularly once the support of her family that she'd been used to was no longer available. She was too young, too self-engrossed and too mentally ill to find any consolation in loving us and looking after us. Her life was completely miserable, and she grew increasingly dependent on pills and alcohol.

My first memories are of around that time, although in fact they're mostly feelings rather than memories of actual incidents. For example, I can remember many occasions when I was afraid and many when I saw blood on my mother's face and tried to block out the sound of her screams. My earliest complete memory is of when I was three and opened the living room door one day just as my father was beating up my mother.

I stood there, frozen to the spot by shock, and he suddenly swung round and screamed at me, 'Hit her! Go on, hit her. She likes it.'

I looked at my mother, who was cowering in an armchair, blood pouring from her nose as she tried to protect her face with her arms, and I was really frightened. But when I looked back at my father, I felt an excitement that was even stronger than my fear, because he'd spoken directly to me, which he never normally did.

How to get his attention was something I often thought about as a child. He never touched me or cuddled me or let me sit on his knee – ever – and I used to fantasise about what it would be like if he treated me more like he treated my brother Chris, holding my hand and speaking to me without anger and dislike in his voice. And that day, as I stood in the doorway of the living room, I thought that this might be my chance at last. Perhaps if I sided with my father against my mother, he'd look at me and realise I was just as good as my brother. Of course, that's how I explain it now, with the benefit of rational thought. At the time, though, I just had a mixture of emotions – fear and pity for my mother, and elation at the thought that, finally, my father was including me in something.

To my undying shame, I clenched my fist, walked across the room to the armchair and hit my already beaten mother.

'Look at that!' my father crowed triumphantly, pushing his face up close to hers. 'Even your own daughter doesn't like you.'

It was almost like getting his approval – for the first time in my life – and it should have felt good. But, somehow, although it was the one thing I'd always longed for, I was miserable, and too guilty to look my whimpering mother in the eyes.

Another early memory is of going into the garden, where my father was drinking with some of his mates. I stood against the wall of the house, watching them and listening to their laughter. I'd probably only been standing there for a minute or two when my father noticed me and called me over to him.

'Stand there,' he commanded, pointing to a spot on the grass near his feet.

I felt a hot flush of excitement: my father was speaking to me without cursing or shouting. I almost threw myself on to the grass in my eagerness to show him how well I could do what he told me.

He grinned at his friends, turned to pick up an empty tea chest and slammed it down over my head, trapping my fingers under one edge and imprisoning me in the dark.

I burst into tears. My fingers were throbbing painfully and I was shocked and frightened. I could hear my father and his friends laughing and I felt humiliated. I'd been stupid to believe that, for the very first time in my life, my father had had anything other than bad intentions towards me.

After a while, he lifted the edge of the tea chest a few inches, releasing my swollen fingers.

'Aw, come on; it was just a joke.' His voice was mocking. 'Okay, then. Out you come.'

He raised the tea chest a little further, but just as I was scrabbling to my feet, he slammed it down again. This time, as well as the muffled sound of laughter, I heard the creaking of wood as he sat down on top of it.

I was frightened of the darkness, and I was frightened of the feeling of not being able to breathe, so by the time my father eventually let me out, I was sobbing hysterically.

'Look at her,' my father sneered to his friends. 'She's nothing but a great big baby.' As he spoke, he pushed me so that I fell on the grass, and as I struggled to get to my feet, he shouted, 'Go on, fuck off back inside the house.'

Still crying, I ran up the garden, away from the sound of the men's scornful, mocking voices. And by the time I reached the back door, my father had already forgotten I existed.

My mother, my brother and I lived in a permanent atmosphere of fear and nervous apprehension. Every day, as the time approached when my father was due home from work, my mother would become tensely anxious and would shout at me to clear up my toys. Sometimes, he'd be in a good mood and she'd be pathetically grateful and relieved. But he could change without warning, and we lived in constant fear of doing something that might irritate or upset him.

One day, he beat up my mother so badly she had to be taken to hospital by ambulance, and he was arrested by the military police. As soon as he was released, he collected me and Chris and drove with us to the hospital. Although he didn't speak to us at all, I could sense the anger radiating from him, and I can still remember his painfully tight grip on my wrist as he marched down the hospital corridor, literally dragging us behind him.

There were other women on the ward, and there must have been nurses, too, although I don't recall seeing them. But not even the presence of other people could shame my father into controlling his fury. He stood beside my mother's bed and screamed abuse at her, while she just sat there crying, her swollen face almost unrecognisable beneath all the cuts and bruises. Then he turned abruptly on his heels, grabbed Chris's hand and stamped off back down the ward.

My mother called after him, pleading, 'Please, Paul. I'm sorry. It wasn't your fault. Please come back.'

I felt really sad for her, until I realised that my father was going to leave without me. I ran after him, begging him to wait for me, but he ignored me and kept on walking away with my brother.

Although my father's physical violence was largely directed towards my mother, he sometimes hurt me, too, and I still have a small, round scar from a cigarette burn he made just below my knee – a permanent reminder of how much he disliked me.

He used to go to the pub almost every night, and my mother resented being left behind to look after Chris and me while he was out having a good time. In reality, though, she was too selfish simply to accept the fact that she had two young children and had to stay at home to look after us. She'd often put us to bed, give us some medicine that made us sleep and then sneak out to a different pub to meet a boyfriend. Although she always made sure she got home before my father, it seems strange for her to have risked him finding out what she was doing, particularly when she was so afraid of him. It was as though she couldn't help herself. Perhaps she was driven by the same devil inside her that made her do things that almost tore her family apart when she was a teenager.

As a child, I didn't know there was anything 'wrong' with my mother, although I *was* aware from a very early age of her manic-depressive episodes.

One night, I was woken up by the sound of someone crying and I lay in the darkness, anxiously listening. I shared a bedroom with Chris, but clearly the crying wasn't coming from him and after few moments he whispered, 'Are you awake? Can you hear it?' He sounded as scared as I was.

The wailing grew louder, until I knew we couldn't simply ignore it.

'We'll have to go and see what it is,' I told my brother, trying to sound braver than I felt. 'We'll be okay if we go together.'

I'm sure he didn't believe that any more than I did, but the only thing more frightening than coming with me would have been for him to stay in the bedroom alone. So he climbed out of bed and felt for my hand in the dark.

I took a deep breath and slowly opened the bedroom door, my heart thumping with terror as I tried not to imagine all the horrifying things that might be on the other side of it. But the landing was empty. We tiptoed along it together, our pyjamas damp with the cold sweat of fear, and crept halfway down the stairs, where we stopped and crouched low so that we could see through the spindles of the banister. We had a clear view of the open living-room door and of a large part of the room itself, and could see a woman pacing up and down, cradling her empty arms as though she was holding a baby, and talking agitatedly between loud, heart-rending sobs.

'Who is that?' I whispered to my brother. 'Is that our mummy?'

'I think so.' Chris's voice was barely audible. 'It...It sort of looks like her...'

I tightened my grasp on his hand and bit my lip to stop myself crying out. I couldn't understand what the woman was saying, and I still wasn't sure whether she was my mother or someone really scary who looked a bit like her. She crossed in front of the open door repeatedly, but never once did she look away from whatever she could see in her arms and notice us. We watched her for a while and then crept silently back up the stairs, climbed into my bed together and held hands tightly until we fell asleep.

MY MOTHER'S PARENTS often came to visit us in those days and when my mother was certain my father couldn't hear her, she'd plead with them to take us away and let us live with them. My grandfather's response was always the same. Although his dislike of my father had grown stronger over the years my parents had been married, he would tell my mother she had to stick it out and make the best of it 'for the sake of the children'. What was more important than anything else, he would tell her, was that my brother and I had two parents. He was wrong, as it turned out, but I think he meant well.

Of course, part of the problem was that my mother had always had a tendency to exaggerate and overdramatise everything. She'd been doing it since she was a small child, and her parents had grown used to never knowing what part of anything she said was fact and what part was fiction. So my grandfather simply didn't realise how miserably hopeless our lives had become.

3

A new beginning

IT WASN'T LONG before something must have happened to make my grandfather change his mind, because one day he arrived at the house with my uncle and told my father, 'That's enough. I'm taking them home with me. They won't be coming back.' He didn't shout or even seem angry. He just spoke in his calm, authoritative way without raising his voice. But I think my father could tell he'd made up his mind and that he was in no mood for arguments.

I could feel my heart thumping, as though it was growing larger with every beat until it started banging against my ribs. Were we really going to escape from the constant threat of my father's violent temper and go to live with my grandparents, who I adored? I didn't dare believe it was true.

It wasn't long, though, before my excitement turned to fear, as it became clear that my father wasn't going to let us go without a fight. I didn't understand why he bothered: I was sure he'd be glad to see my mother and me leave, although I knew he'd be sorry about losing my brother – for a while, at least. So perhaps it was just because he liked to be in charge. He always insisted on being the person issuing the orders, whatever the situation, and I suppose it was the fact that my grandfather had taken control out of his hands that made him so aggressive.

My father was a bully and, like all bullies, only abused those who couldn't fight back. So he didn't try to vent his anger and frustration on my grandfather or my uncle. Instead, he started screaming at my mother, who, for once secure in the knowledge that there was someone there to protect her, screamed back at him.

'It's okay.' My grandfather could see that I was frightened, and he laid a large, comforting hand on my shoulder. 'Just go and put on your shoes and coat. Take Chris with you.'

A few minutes later, I walked out of the front door of my home and stood waiting to be told what to do next. My father was standing by the gate, still shouting and swearing, and when he saw me, he walked back up the path, bent down until his face was level with mine and shouted, 'That fucking doll was bought with *my* money, and that makes it *my* fucking doll. You don't own a single thing. So you won't be taking a single thing with you.'

Thin threads of his saliva spattered across my face as he spoke, and I could feel his hot, stale breath on my cheek. I tightened my grip on my doll, Sally, and tried to tuck her under the open front of my coat. But he snatched her easily from my hands, pulling her away from me with one sharp tug and tossing her on the ground between us.

'Good God, man!' My uncle sounded shocked and angry. 'Surely you can let the child keep her doll!'

My father smiled a slow, smug smile that didn't reach his eyes, and then ground the heel of his boot into Sally's face.

I was still sobbing hysterically when my mother came flying out of the house shouting, 'You fucking bastard!' For a split-second I thought she was finally going to speak up on my behalf. But when I looked at her face I could see that her anger was more an expression of how much she was enjoying the drama of it all than of any feelings of sympathy for me. She was probably already imagining telling the story at the pub. She loved describing the terrible life she had to put up with, not least because the more shocking the story – suitably embellished – the sorrier people felt for her and the more drinks they bought her.

The woman who lived in the house next door had come out into her garden when all the noise started, and she was standing, openly watching, with one hand resting on the fence and the fingers of the other holding a cigarette to her lips.

My father turned towards her. 'We've got some toys for your kids,' he said, reaching into the open bag my mother had dumped beside the front door and pulling out a teddy bear and a red-painted steam engine, my brother's pride and joy. 'Anna and Chris don't want them any more.'

As he walked towards her, I began dragging toys out of the bag and trying to stuff them into my pockets and under my coat, although I was sure the woman wouldn't take them, because it was obvious that what my father said wasn't true. But when I looked up again, the neighbour was smirking as she reached eagerly across the fence to snatch the things my father was holding out to her.

My uncle clenched his fists and took a step towards my father, as if he was going to hit him. I felt a sudden thrill of satisfaction at the thought that someone was finally going to stand up to my father in our defence, but my grandfather laid a hand on my uncle's arm and said gruffly, 'Leave it. Let's just get them out of here.' So, instead, my uncle took the small suitcase my mother was holding and threw it into the boot of my grandfather's car, along with a couple of carrier bags of hastily collected clothes. Then my brother and I clambered on to the back seat and we drove away, my mother still cursing my father as she leaned dangerously out of the open window beside her, and my father shouting and gesticulating furiously from the pavement outside our house.

Leaving our home and our father was a horrible, traumatic experience for many reasons, and it left me and my brother – at the ages of just four and two and a half – without a single familiar or loved possession. What I didn't know on that day, though, was that it was to be the beginning of the two happiest years of my life.

I'D KNOWN FROM a very early age that my father actively disliked me, and although I didn't realise it at the time, there was nothing I would ever be able to do – no instance of good behaviour or amazing achievement – that would make him change his mind. My mother's attitude towards me, however, was more one of indifference: I was a nuisance and an inconvenience to her and, most of the time, she was happy simply to ignore me, as long as I didn't get in her way. And she never let me forget that the reason my father treated her so badly was because I was a girl, rather than the son he'd wanted. I knew I was a disappointment to them both, and at the age of four I was already convinced that I was as worthless as they so often told me I was.

Therefore, particularly in contrast to the first four years of my life, living with my grandparents was an unimaginable revelation as I slowly discovered what it felt like to be loved and what a difference that feeling can make to a child's life. In their large, comfortable house in a quiet road in an affluent area of town, Chris and I became completely different children. We idolised our grandparents and loved our aunts and uncles, and they in turn made us feel special and important.

From being a timid, uncared-for and anxious child, I became a well-dressed, well-spoken little girl who made friends quickly when I started at the local school. For the first time in my life, I felt I fitted in somewhere. I'd never before experienced consistency and stability, and I loved being part of a respectable family and living *within* a community, rather than at the edge, always watching and feeling excluded. And I loved not having to be afraid and wary all the time. It was as though my grandparents had built an invisible protective bubble around me, enclosing within it all the things I wanted to be part of and making it impossible for anything or anyone to hurt me.

The very best part of every day was the early morning, when my grandmother came into the bedroom I shared with my mother – when she bothered to come home at night – and whispered to me, 'Wake up, sleepy head. God has blessed us with another beautiful day.' Or, sometimes, 'God has sent rain to make the farmers smile.'

As she tiptoed out of the room again, I'd jump out of bed, quickly get washed and dressed and then almost tumble down the stairs in my eagerness to reach the kitchen, where I'd sit at the table and wait for her. As everyone else rushed to get ready for work, my grandmother and I would eat toast and marmalade and talk to each other. It was a wonderful way to start the day and I'd always leave for school full of confidence in the knowledge that my grandmother loved me, and therefore I was someone special.

Having been used to being considered an irritating nuisance (by my mother) and a completely worthless waste of space (by my father), I'd always assumed there was something wrong with me, something I didn't understand that made me unlovable. So I could hardly believe that someone as wonderful as my grandmother actually wanted to sit and eat her breakfast with me every morning.

During the two years we lived with our grandparents, Chris and I built very special bonds with them. They became the parents we'd never had and, perhaps most importantly of all, they made us see that there was another way of living. Until then, like all children, I'd simply accepted the hand I'd been dealt. I'd been completely unaware that other people's lives might be different from my own. If I *had* ever thought about it, I'm sure I'd have assumed that all mummies got drunk and that all daddies shouted and swore and punched them until they cried and blood ran down their faces. But living with my grandparents and having close contact with my aunts and uncles made me realise that some people are kind to each other, that they live together happily, without screaming and fighting, and that maybe it was possible to choose what sort of life you wanted to have.

My grandfather still worked in construction and he often had to go abroad on contracts, sometimes for weeks at a time. My grandmother would go with him, as she'd always done, and so would my brother and I during the school holidays. During term time, however, we stayed at home in my grandparents' house, 'looked after' by our mother, although it was actually our aunts and uncles who fed, clothed and cared for us. My mother's sisters and brothers had countless arguments with her as they tried to make her understand her responsibilities towards us. But however furious and frustrated they became with her, they were always good to my brother and me and always careful to make sure we knew they weren't angry with us.

It seemed that my mother always had her finger on a self-destruct button. When she left my father, she'd had a choice between her children and her love of alcohol, and she'd chosen the latter. Surprisingly, though, considering the amount she drank, she somehow managed to hold down a job in an office. She was young and attractive, and there was no shortage of men willing to pay for her evenings out. So she rarely came home after work other than to wash and change her clothes before flying out of the front door again.

I don't remember ever missing my father or wishing he was there and, fortunately, during that time neither he nor my mother really figured in my life. They'd both become strangers to me and I was happy for my new life to revolve around my grandparents, aunts and uncles.

My mother had impressed upon my brother and me as soon as we moved in with my grandparents that we were never to call her Mum or try to hold her hand in public. She told us she didn't want her new friends to know she had children. I didn't really understand what she meant, and it felt as though she was ashamed of us. I accepted it, though, as I accepted everything, and for a while I was satisfied just to run to the front door to greet her as soon as I heard the sound of her footsteps coming up the garden path. Eventually, however, after repeated rebuffs and the hurt and disappointment that brought hot tears to my eyes each time she flicked her wrist irritably to loosen my grip on her hand, my eagerness to see her dwindled to a self-protective indifference. And then I barely lifted my head to look as she flung open the front door and ran up the stairs, shedding dirty clothes in her wake.

Sometimes, I'd be playing in the garden with a friend when my mother came home from work and walked straight past us without any sign of acknowledgement. Then my stomach would start to churn as I waited for the argument that always started as soon as she set foot inside the house.

'You just don't want me to enjoy myself,' my mother would scream. 'You can't bear the thought that I've got friends. If you don't want to look after the kids, send them back to their useless bastard of a father and let's see how he likes not being able to go out in the evenings.'

My grandmother would sound angry and there'd be a sharp tone of exasperation in her voice that I only ever heard when she was arguing with my mother, as she answered, 'For pity's sake, Judith! You haven't been home for the last three nights. And now you've only come to get a change of clothes. Surely it isn't too much to hope that you'd want to spend just a few minutes with your own children?'

Then someone would remember we were playing in the garden and a window would bang shut, muffling the sound of their voices.

I'd continue to play as if nothing had happened, avoiding looking at my friend so that I didn't have to see the embarrassment on her face. And, after a while, the front door would be wrenched open and my mother would march past us again, before setting off down the road towards the pub, while I blinked back my tears and pretended I didn't care.

I did care, though – at least, to begin with – and one day I ran down the road after her, asking where she was going and begging her to take me with her. But she just kept on walking, waving her arm to brush me aside and hissing at me angrily, 'Get back home to your grand-mother.' So I stood and watched her walk away, finally accepting the fact that the only thing that really mattered to her was drinking with her friends.

As well as being an alcoholic, my mother became addicted to laxatives and diet pills and developed bulimia, making herself sick every time she ate or drank anything. I grew used to the circus of emotions that accompanied her wherever she went. Nothing about her was ever calm or reasonable; every aspect of her life was steeped in the drama of confrontation and resentment. And then, when I was five years old, I came home from school one day and knew immediately that something more serious than usual was wrong.

My grandmother was waiting for me at the front door, her face red and blotchy. I felt my heart lurch with fear, because it seemed that in the space of just one day, since I'd left the house for school that morning, she'd suddenly become old. She bent down to hug me and then took my hand and led me into the kitchen, where she pulled out two chairs from beside the kitchen table and said, 'Sit down for a minute, Anna. There's something I have to tell you.'

She turned to look out of the kitchen window and then dabbed impatiently at her eyes with the corner of her apron before turning back towards me again.

'Your mummy isn't very well,' she told me. 'She's had to go to the hospital.'

She must have seen the alarmed expression on my face, and she took hold of my hand as she added hastily, 'She's going to be all right, though. She may have to stay in the hospital for a little while. But there's nothing for you to worry about. Everything here will be just the way it always is. You and Chris will be fine.'

For the first time in my life, I wasn't sure I believed what my grandmother was telling me. If there was nothing to worry about, why did she look so anxious and tired and as though she'd been crying?

'Can we go and see her?' I asked, half-dreading the answer.

'No, not for a while at least,' my grandmother replied. 'Children aren't allowed at this sort of hospital.'

She patted the back of my hand and then stood up abruptly, placing her chair back under the table and looking out of the window again with sad eyes.

The next morning, I was walking very slowly down the stairs, wondering why my grandmother hadn't woken me up in time to have breakfast with her, as she always did, when I heard my grandfather's voice. He was in the living room, talking to someone I couldn't see through the partially open door, and my attention was caught by his hushed, almost whispered tone. As I stopped to listen, I heard him say, 'It was a terrible thing to witness.'

For a moment, I thought he was crying, but I knew that wasn't possible, because my grandfather never cried.

'We called the ambulance, although we thought we were too late. I keep asking myself, why? Why would Judith try to commit suicide?'

It felt as though the hallway had started to spin around me and I gripped the banister tightly to stop myself tumbling down the stairs. I knew what suicide meant – it meant trying to kill yourself – and I knew it was a very bad thing to do, because only God could decide when you were born and when you died.

My mother was in hospital for several weeks, and my brother and I didn't go to see her there at all – not on that occasion and not on any of the other occasions during the next two years when she was taken away in an ambulance.

By the time she came home after that first incident, I'd worked myself up into an almost hysterical state of anxiety about what I overheard my grandfather say that day. It wasn't until some time later, though, that I finally summoned the courage to ask my mother the question that had been tormenting me for so long: 'Do people go to heaven if they commit suicide?'

My mother just shrugged and said, 'No, apparently not.'

It was confirmation of exactly what I'd suspected. But, even so, it was a terrible shock. I simply couldn't understand why my mother would try to do something that would make God angry. And I didn't dare think about where she *would* go if she didn't go to heaven. For years, I worried about what would happen to her if she ever succeeded in killing herself, or, if she didn't, how God would view the fact that she'd tried.

After that first attempt, she spent a lot of time in hospital. I didn't really understand why until much later, when I realised that it was usually because she'd tried to kill herself again or been sectioned under the Mental Health Act when her alcoholism or manic-depression tipped the precarious balance of her mind too far.

On one of the occasions when my mother was in hospital, one of my aunts started dating a new boyfriend, and my grandmother insisted she must take Chris and me with her on all their dates – including the very first one. Looking back on it now, it seems very unfair. But I don't remember my aunt or her boyfriend ever complaining about it, and the fact that he wasn't put off altogether by our presence certainly says something about how keen he was on my aunt. He was a kind, generous man, and they were both very good to us, taking us with them on picnics in the woods and to the beach, and treating us as though we were their own children. In fact, I used to pretend they were my parents, and Chris and I couldn't believe our luck when our aunt's boyfriend later became our uncle. I'd dream about being adopted by them and living with them for ever, and it seems that at one point I might have come quite close to getting my wish.

Children know when the adults they live with are keeping secrets, and I became good at tuning in to the whispered conversations that stopped or changed abruptly to hearty cheerfulness as soon as someone noticed I was there. One day, when my mother had just been sectioned and was in hospital again, I heard one of my uncles talking to my aunt.

'Whether it's her *fault* or not that she's ill is beside the point,' my uncle said angrily. 'The fact remains that she's not a fit mother. Those kids deserve better, and Mum and Dad need to have the right to make decisions about their lives, because Judith sure as hell doesn't want to be bothered.'

By piecing together the fragments of conversation I overheard, I learned that when my grandmother and uncle had gone to see my mother at the hospital, they'd tried to get her to sign adoption papers for me and my brother. But the psychiatrist had discovered what they were doing and had almost literally thrown them out, furious with them for attempting to coerce his vulnerable patient into giving away her children. The psychiatrist was probably right to do what he did – from a legal point of view, at least – although perhaps he wouldn't have felt quite so outraged if he'd known what it was like to live with my mother, or if he'd been able to see into our future.

Paradoxically, it seems that although we were nothing but a nuisance to my mother when we stood in the way of her going out and having a good time, she felt differently when she was in hospital. I'd like to think that somewhere deep down inside her she loved me, but I know she didn't really want me. Although she continued to refuse to give us up, it was largely because she liked having the upper hand and took pleasure in *not* doing whatever people wanted her to do – particularly when those people were the members of her own family.

Another overheard conversation took place shortly after my mother had spent four months in a psychiatric hospital and was telling one of her friends how easy it had been to get hold of alcohol there.

'God, you'd need a few drinks before you did the dirty

with *some* of the night staff,' she said, and they both laughed. 'There was this one male nurse…'

I crept away, unwilling to hear the details she was about to describe. I didn't know whether what she was saying was true or whether she was just showing off to her friend. That was always a problem with my mother: her love of drama – and perhaps, also, her refusal to admit that anything about her life was dull and mundane – made her almost incapable of relating any story without gross exaggeration. What I wasn't in any doubt about, however, was the fact that she'd have managed somehow to get hold of drink while she was in hospital, because there was nothing more important to her than a steady supply of alcohol and I knew she'd do whatever it took to get it. She'd been resolute in her refusal to give my brother and me up for adoption by her family; but I knew that if she had a choice between us and drink, she'd have abandoned us without a second thought.

During one period when she was sectioned, she made friends with an anorexic girl who had hair down to her waist and who later died in hospital. By the time my mother came home, she'd become fixated on the idea that I must grow my hair. However, in her usual spirit of always having to do everything to the nth degree, she announced that *my* hair must be allowed to grow not just to my waist, like her friend's, but until it touched my feet, and she would fly into a rage if anyone ever suggested I should have it cut.

I wasn't consulted, of course, and I hated it. As my hair grew, it became more and more difficult to manage, and the daily ritual of tying it up and plaiting it – a process that tugged painfully at the skin on my scalp – seemed to take hours. Then, one day, I told my mother that my friends at school said they thought I should get it cut. I knew that the topic of my hair was dangerous ground on which to be treading, but the feeling that I looked ridiculous had finally given me the courage to say something.

I was always on the alert with my mother, because, however 'normal' she might appear when she was talking to you, her mood could change instantly, without any warning. Even so, I was taken by surprise by the violence of her response. She grabbed my shoulders, her fingertips digging into my flesh so painfully that the bruises they made were still clearly visible several days later. I turned my head away from her instinctively, thinking she was going to hit me. But instead she screamed hysterically, 'What right have your fucking bitch friends to tell you to get your hair cut? What kind of stupid bitch are you to take any notice of them? Haven't you got a fucking mind of your own?'

Through the shock and fear I felt a rush of indignant resentment. Growing my hair had been *her* idea, not mine. So, from her point of view, it was just as well if I *didn't* have a mind of my own. However, I knew better than to argue; instead, I looked at my feet and waited for her tirade of furious abuse to stop. I didn't understand why it mattered so much to her, but clearly it did, and I had no reason to doubt the fact that she would get her own way with regard to my hair, just as she did with almost everything else.

As my hair grew longer, my mother took every possible opportunity to parade me in front of her drunken friends, boasting about it as though it was some great achievement of her own and telling them that *her* daughter wasn't going to be 'like all the rest of the bitches with short hair'. In the pub, she'd sneer drunkenly at the mothers of other girls and say, 'You needn't bother bringing that bitch of a daughter of yours to the pub. No one's going to notice her when my Anna's here.' Everyone was used to her volatile, aggressive moods and no one dared confront her. They'd simply nod their agreement – and then corner me or my brother later and tell us how crazy our mother was. As if we didn't know!

In the past, I'd often wished my mother would pay some attention to me, instead of concentrating all her energies on getting drunk. But this wasn't the sort of attention I'd wanted. She still didn't notice *me*; I was just a vehicle for her new fixation, which had arisen because of a dead girl I'd never met. I hated having long hair, and

I hated being different from all my friends, but I knew it was pointless trying to reason with my self-absorbed, angry and unreasonable mother.

In fact, I spent very little time with my mother during the time we lived with my grandparents, except when they were away and she couldn't find anyone else to palm us off on. On the rare occasions she had to look after us she'd be forced to take us with her to the pub, where her version of parental care involved making us sit outside on our own for virtually the whole weekend while she drank herself into a stupor inside. The pubs she went to didn't have gardens or family areas; they were always in the middle of town, and we'd sit on their doorsteps, on the street, from opening time until they closed, or until someone realised where we were and came to take us away.

On the 'good' days, we'd go to a pub where my mother knew the landlord and where my brother and I would be allowed to sit in the back room. We knew that we mustn't disturb her for any reason; if we did, she'd thrash us when we got home. So we just sat there, for hour after miserable hour, while she moaned to anyone in the bar who'd listen and told them about what a difficult life she had, wallowing in their sympathy and drinking the drinks of consolation they bought for her.

As usual, we were under very strict instructions not to

tell our grandparents – or anyone else – where we'd been all day. And we didn't, because we knew there was always a high price to pay for disobeying our mother.

Fortunately, though, the days with our mother were outnumbered by the days we spent with my grandparents, aunts and uncles, who were very good to Chris and me. My mother's sisters and brothers looked after us on the many, many occasions when my mother dumped us on them so that she could go off and drink and exert her 'right' to enjoy herself. Chris and I must have been a burden to them, but they never made us feel like one. They fed and clothed us and made us believe we were loved and wanted, and I'll always be grateful to them for everything they did for me.

Perhaps most importantly of all, they were strong, positive influences in the negative atmosphere my mother always created around her, and they taught me that life could be different from – and unimaginably better than – the life I'd always known. In some respects, though, that was a lesson that made it even harder to accept the miserable, degrading new life I was about to live.

4

This is my daddy

MY PARENTS WERE divorced soon after we went to live with my grandparents and Chris and I rarely saw or heard from my father. In fact, I don't remember even thinking about him. Sometimes, my brother would cry and scream at my mother, 'I don't want you. I want my daddy.' And she'd shout back at him, 'If you want your father so much, you can fucking go and live with him.' To Chris, though, the words weren't simply something he'd say to try to get back at my mother when she was being mean; he really did miss his dad. I couldn't understand how he felt, and it wasn't until many years later that I realised his experience of living with our father was completely different from my own, because he'd had an opportunity to develop a relationship with him. My father had always wanted a son, and as much as he was able to love anyone he loved my brother, whereas I could never form any type of bond with him because, for some unknown reason, he hated and distrusted all women, including his own mother.

But although I didn't miss my father, I never lost hope that one day he'd change his mind about me and see that I *was* worthy of his attention. So, when I was five years old and he invited Chris and me to his sister's wedding, I was really excited.

When the big day finally arrived, I had breakfast with my grandmother as usual, and although she talked and listened to me as she always did, she seemed tense and distracted. She had a look in her eyes that I'd learned to recognise as meaning something bad had happened, but I decided I must be mistaken, because the day ahead was an exciting one.

After breakfast, I ran upstairs to put on my best party frock and then twirled round the kitchen to show my grandmother how I looked.

'You look beautiful, darling,' she told me. Then she turned away and started clattering dishes into the sink, so that her voice was slightly muffled as she added, 'Just be careful.'

For a moment I was puzzled, but then I realised she was worried in case I made a mess of my best dress. Although it wasn't like her to be emotional about something so relatively trivial, I knew that there was no accounting for the things that upset adults. So I hugged her extra tightly, assured her I'd take the greatest of care, and then ran to the living room to sit on the windowsill and wait for my father.

What I was looking forward to most of all was showing off my father to my new uncle – the patient, kind man who'd recently married my aunt. He and all my other uncles were at the house that day, although it wasn't until years later that it dawned on me they'd gathered there in case there was any trouble.

As soon as I saw my father approaching the house, I ran to open the front door, and was chattering so excitedly I barely noticed the lack of enthusiasm in his greeting. Grabbing his hand, I almost dragged him into the living room, where I raised my arm as if displaying some rare treasure and told my newest uncle proudly, '*This* is my daddy!'

My father held out his hand. But, to my horror, my uncle ignored it, giving instead a curt nod of his head as he said, in a cold, serious voice I didn't recognise, 'Hello, Paul.'

I felt a flush of hot, embarrassed disappointment rise from my toes to the top of my head. How could my uncle – who was always cheerful and nice to everyone – be so rude? Surely he was excited to be meeting my daddy? So what possible reason could he have for sounding unfriendly and for not shaking the hand that was offered to him?

My father just shrugged. It seemed he was as eager to leave the house as my family were to see him go, and it wasn't long before Chris and I were piling into his car and setting off with him in the direction of his mother's house, which was where we would be staying that night, after the wedding.

Since I'd been told that we were going to stay with my father's mother – my other grandmother – I'd been trying to remember what she looked like, but without success. So I'd settled on imagining she'd be just like my mother's mother, whereas in fact she was about as different from her as it was possible to be. When Chris and I clambered out of the car at the end of our journey, she said 'Hello' to Chris and then just glanced at me with eyes that didn't smile like my 'real' grandmother's did.

When my father took us upstairs to put away our things, he opened the door of a dismal, uncarpeted room that seemed to be full of beds, like a dormitory. I sat down on the bed nearest the door and tried a couple of tentative bounces.

'Get off there,' my father snapped immediately, hitting my shoulder with his fist. 'Those are your uncles' beds. That's yours.' He turned and pointed to a small, blanket-covered mattress on the floor.

I knew my uncles all had homes of their own, but thought that perhaps they were going to sleep at their mother's house after the wedding. I was about to ask my father about it when he said, 'It'll be just you in here. Chris will be in my room.' Chris pulled a face and I felt a thrill of pride at the thought that *I* was the one who was trusted enough to sleep alone in a special little bed in a room normally reserved for my father's brothers.

I can't remember anything about the wedding itself, except that afterwards, in the evening, we went to the reception. We were driven there by one of my uncles; my father sat beside him in the passenger seat and Chris and I sat together in the back of the car. Every time we stopped at traffic lights, I'd make Chris laugh by knocking on the window to attract the attention of the people in whatever car pulled up beside us. Then, with a suitably anguished expression on my face, I'd mouth the words, 'Help! We've been kidnapped.'

Kidnapped was a new word to me and one I only vaguely understood. I'd learned it just a few days previously when I'd overheard my grandparents discussing the possibility that my father might be intending to 'kidnap' Chris and me if we were allowed to go to his sister's wedding. Judging by the anxiety the discussion had caused my grandmother, being kidnapped was something pretty serious and something you wouldn't want to happen to someone you loved. Other than that, though, I had no real idea what it meant.

Nevertheless, each time the car stopped, I repeated my charade, and then, as the lights changed and the traffic started moving again, Chris and I collapsed in quickly stifled giggles. It was becoming increasingly difficult to keep a straight face while enacting my mini-drama, but I managed to do so one last time when we pulled up at traffic lights beside two men in a large, black car. Suddenly, the passenger door flew open and one of the men jumped out, tapped on the window beside my uncle and called, 'Open up, mate.'

My uncle turned towards him in surprise.

'Open the window,' the man said again, slowly this time and with a note of aggression in his voice.

My uncle looked at him for a moment and then wound the window down a couple of inches.

'They your kids?' the man asked.

He was standing very close to the car, the fingers of one hand hooked over the top of my uncle's window, and he looked enormous. I held my breath and wondered just how angry my father and uncle were going to be. Clearly, being kidnapped was something even more serious than I'd realised.

As the cars behind us sounded their horns, anxious to get through the lights before they turned red again, Chris and I answered the man's questions and apologised for being what my father later called 'fucking stupid'. Finally, the man seemed satisfied and he got back into the car with his friend and they drove away.

Throughout our interrogation, my father had turned in his seat and glared silently at my brother and me. But as soon as the man had gone and we were driving along in the car again, he released all his pent-up fury. Luckily though, his opportunity to shout was short-lived, because a few minutes later we arrived at the hall attached to the pub where the wedding reception was being held.

The next morning, I woke up in the little bed in my uncles' room with my body covered in what appeared to be crusty, foul-smelling scabs. Horrified, I tiptoed into the bathroom, looked in the mirror and began to cry. With my heart pounding, I tried to wash them off, but it was as though they were glued to my skin. I started picking at them frantically with my fingernails, and had managed to loosen one or two of them when I heard my grandmother calling me to come down for breakfast. I felt sick. I thought I must have developed some terrible disease in the night, and I knew that my father hated illness of any sort. I was sure he'd be furious with me. It was the first time he'd seen me in months, and the fact that I was now covered in horrible, stinking scabs would simply serve to confirm his opinion that I was nothing but trouble.

I crept down the stairs and stood silently in the doorway that led into the kitchen, where my grandmother, father and brother were already sitting at the table eating their breakfast. I was too embarrassed and humiliated to go into the room, and when they eventually looked up and saw me, I could see genuine alarm in Chris's eyes. I began to sob. But instead of the tirade of abuse I was expecting from my father, he just smiled at my grandmother in a private sort of way, pointed towards a place that had been set for me at the far end of the table and said, 'Sit down and eat your breakfast.'

Chris looked at my father in amazement, as surprised as I was by his non-reaction. Then he wrinkled his nose in disgust at the smell that had accompanied me into the room.

Suddenly, my father smiled a strange, humourless smile and leapt to his feet shrieking, 'What the fuck is that revolting stink? Jesus, girl, is that coming from you?'

I felt an involuntary spasm contort my face, making my eyes snap shut, and a shudder like an electric shock passed through my whole body.

My father laid his hand on my brother's shoulder in a subtle indication of the fact that the two of them were united against me and said, with a sneer, 'What's the matter with your sister, Chris? Does she always stink like this?'

Although Chris wriggled in his chair, trying to edge it further away from where I was sitting, he didn't answer.

Perhaps he didn't want to be on my father's side, or perhaps he was afraid – as I was – that I'd caught some horrible disease. I couldn't understand, though, why neither my father nor his mother seemed worried about what was wrong with me. At home, my 'real' grandmother would have placed a cool hand on my forehead to see if I had a temperature. And then, talking to me in her calm, reassuring voice, she'd have led me back up the stairs and tucked me up in bed while my grandfather made a phone call to the doctor.

At my 'other' grandmother's house, though, I just sat at the table, with no appetite for any breakfast, and tried to endure the taunts until the time came for my father to drive us home.

In the car, my father made me sit on newspapers, which he'd spread in a thick layer across the back seat. Then he opened all the windows and told Chris to sit beside him in the front. My cheeks burned with shame as my father kept up a steady stream of cruel jokes and comments all the way back to my grandparents' house. When we finally arrived and he stopped in front of the house, I couldn't get out of the car fast enough. Then the father I had so looked forward to seeing said goodbye to my brother and, without a word to me, drove away.

I ran up the path ahead of Chris, anxious to show the terrible scabs to my grandparents, who I knew would give me the sympathy and reassurance I so desperately needed. When my grandmother opened the front door, I burst into tears and she stood for a moment with an expression of shock on her face that confirmed my own worst fears. Then she called to my grandfather as she pulled me gently into the house, and I stood in the hallway, sobbing loudly, while my grandparents examined me and asked me questions, their dismay turning slowly to anger.

I had never seen my grandmother as furious as she was that day – not even on any of the occasions when my mother was ranting and raving at her and my grandmother was trying to make her 'see some sense'. It was anger that was fully justified, because it turned out that the evil-smelling 'scabs' covering my body were excrement and that the little bed I'd been so proud to sleep in belonged to my other grandmother's ancient, incontinent dog.

That was the last time during my childhood I was ever allowed to see my father. I didn't forget him, though, because my mother talked about him constantly, particularly about how it was his hatred of *me* that had caused him to treat *her* so badly. According to my mother – the one person who should have loved me, come what may – every bad thing that had ever happened to her was due to my birth and to the fact that my father hadn't wanted a girl. I was a worthless, vindictive little bitch who should never have been born, the root of all her problems and the reason she was drinking herself to death. And it was me – not her – who was responsible for all the many miserable, negative aspects of her life.

Over the next few years, my mother's drunken, rambling, tearful rants were just one of many humiliations for me. I could never confide in her, or tell her anything personal at all, because she had absolutely no respect for my privacy. Every single aspect of our lives became a topic for general discussion, although, in her eyes, the 'best' stories were the ones that were embarrassing or pitiable enough to encourage people to buy sympathy drinks for her. She'd happily relate the most confidential details about us as she bemoaned her lot to anyone in the pub who'd listen, which meant that every sleazy, drunken, low-life loser my mother befriended knew how vulnerable and defenceless we were. And they all took their cue from her and treated me with abusive disdain, even in my own home.

My mother's resentment of me underpinned her attitude towards me throughout my childhood. She and my father considered me worthless, and for years I wished for her sake that I hadn't been born. If she'd just had my brother, I felt that she and my father would have lived happily together, he'd never have treated her so badly, and she wouldn't have had to turn to drink and pills in an attempt to blot out the unacceptable truths of her life. In reality, though, I was just a scapegoat, and all the things she blamed me for were really the result of her own selfish irresponsibility.

What saved me, however, was the love of my grandparents, aunts and uncles. Although it couldn't completely compensate for my parents' blatant dislike of me, it did help me not to mind so much. Sometimes, after having had to listen to a prolonged bout of my mother's catalogue of complaints against me, I'd cheer myself up with the thought that someone as wonderful as my grandmother wouldn't love someone as horrible and useless as my mother believed me to be. I couldn't quite manage to convince myself that my mother's opinion of me was wrong, but there was at least a possibility that it might be. My grandmother was the single most important person in my life, and I knew that as long as I lived with her, I'd be all right, whatever my mother said or did.

AT THE AGE of six, after two years of living with my grandparents, I was confident and happy. But that was about to change.

My grandfather was working away from home on a contract, and for some reason my grandmother hadn't gone with him. So she and my youngest aunt were in the house when I was woken up one night by a strange noise. I lay in bed listening, trying to identify the sound. At first, still confused by sleep, I thought it might be my grandmother singing. But she had a good voice and although it did sound a bit like her, I realised after a few moments that it was really more like wailing than singing.

'What is it?' My heart seemed to stop beating as my brother appeared like a ghost in my bedroom doorway.

'I think it's someone crying,' I answered, still hoping I might be in the middle of a very realistic dream.

Suddenly, the crying stopped, and someone screamed, in what was unmistakably my grandmother's voice, 'No! Please, no,' and then, 'Anna!'

I wanted to shut my eyes and cover my ears to block out the terrible sound of my grandmother's distress. But I loved her more than anything else in the world, and I knew I couldn't just ignore her when she had called my name. Trembling with fear, I slid out of my bed, reached out to take hold of my brother's hand and crept down the stairs with him.

As we stood huddled together by the open kitchen door, I could see my aunt leaning against the sink, one arm raised in front of her face. My grandmother was near the back door, trying to fend off my mother, who was standing very close in front of her, making quick, jabbing motions towards her with a carving knife.

'They're *my* fucking children,' my mother shouted, suddenly lunging forward and drawing the tip of the knife along my grandmother's arm. 'And if I want to take my fucking children to live somewhere else, you can't stop me.'

I tried to stifle a whimper as a line of dark-coloured blood began to trickle towards my grandmother's wrist. Immediately, my mother spun round towards the open door, slamming her fist down on the kitchen work surface and shouting, 'Get your shoes and coats! We're leaving.'

My brother tightened his grip on my hand and we both began to cry.

'Stop snivelling,' my mother snapped, taking a few quick steps towards us and grasping my shoulders roughly as she propelled me back up the stairs. 'We're going to live somewhere else. It'll be fun. It's an adventure!'

She was drunk and her words were slurred and unconvincing. In any case, who in their right mind would want to go on the kind of adventure that began with their mother attacking their grandmother with a knife? It was obvious that my grandmother had been trying to persuade my mother to leave us behind. But my mother was determined, and when she was determined there was no point anyone arguing with her or trying to make her see sense.

A few moments later, still in our nightclothes, with our bare feet crammed into our shoes and our arms shoved hastily into the sleeves of our coats, Chris and I followed our mother back down the stairs, where our aunt and grandmother were huddled together in the kitchen doorway, holding each other and crying softly.

'Please, Judith,' my grandmother whispered. 'Please don't take the children. Why don't you come back for them tomorrow, when you're feeling better?'

'Because I want to take them *now*, you old witch,' my mother shouted. She staggered slightly as she spoke, lurching towards the kitchen doorway as she tried to steady herself, and causing her mother and sister to back hastily away from her.

'Go! Go!' my mother snapped at my brother and me, opening the front door and pushing us out ahead of her into the darkness. As we stumbled down the garden path and out through the gate on to the pavement, my mother hissed at me, 'Don't bother looking back at the old bitch.' But I couldn't help myself. Glancing quickly over my shoulder, I could see my beloved grandmother standing in the front doorway, leaning against my aunt and sobbing as though her heart would break. Then, gripping Chris's hand, I followed my mother's swaying path down the road.

We seemed to have been walking for hours – although we were probably only a few streets away from my grandparents' house – when I plucked up the courage to ask where we were going.

'We're going to live with Carl,' my mother told me, in an exaggeratedly cheerful tone. 'You'll like him.' She concentrated for a moment on negotiating her way around a post box before adding, 'I met him at the pub' – as if that might be a surprise to anyone who knew her – and then, 'You're going to have to behave yourselves, though, and remember that you're bloody lucky he's prepared to let you come and live with us.'

I didn't feel bloody lucky. I felt as though the most terrible thing I could ever have imagined was about to happen to me. But I was wrong, because the reality turned out to be far, far worse than anything I could possibly have imagined.

5

Carl: the end of the new beginning

WE TRUDGED DOWN one cold, deserted, dimly lit street after another, until my mother finally stopped on the pavement in front of a large, imposing brick house and then pushed us impatiently up the path ahead of her. I looked around me at the house's neat, well-maintained front garden and felt a flicker of optimism. Perhaps, for once in her life, my mother had found a decent boyfriend. Maybe Carl was completely different from all the other drunks and low-lifes who were the only people she ever seemed to know. He certainly lived somewhere that was even smarter than my grandparents' house, smarter, in fact, than anywhere I'd ever been with my mother.

As she lifted the polished brass knocker and rapped twice on the front door, I took a step backwards to stand behind her. But she reached round and grabbed the sleeve of my coat, pulling me back beside her again. At that moment, a light came on in the hallway, illuminating the stained glass in the long, narrow windows on either side of the door, which was opened by a grey-haired man wearing a striped dressing gown and leather slippers.

'The kids and I have had a bit of a mishap,' my mother told him, putting her arms affectionately around our shoulders and speaking slowly to try to mask the slur in her voice. Then she added, in what sounded like an embarrassing parody of the way someone posh might have spoken, 'I need to call my friend to give us a lift. Would it be an awful inconvenience if we used your phone?'

It had seemed too good to be true, and it was. My mother didn't know the people who lived in the house. She wanted to make a phone call and she'd chosen to knock on that door simply because, unlike most of the other houses in the surrounding streets, there were still lights on in some of its downstairs rooms.

My heart sank. But the man must have seen how miserable and exhausted Chris and I were and taken pity on us, because he stepped back into the long, high-ceilinged hallway and stood, smiling slightly at us, while my mother made her phone call. Then we waited on the pavement for Carl to arrive in his car, and he drove us to the grim, run-down terraced house where he had his lodgings.

What I couldn't understand for a long time after that was why my mother took Chris and me with her. It certainly wasn't because she loved us and couldn't bear to be parted from us as she set out on her new life with Carl. In fact, she knew almost nothing about us; she'd never tried to get to know us and she had no interest in our likes and dislikes. And if someone had offered to buy us in exchange for providing her with a year's supply of alcohol – which, admittedly, would have been quite a substantial offer – she'd have sold us without a second thought.

Later, I realised that taking us to live with them had probably been Carl's idea. He must have been aware of my mother's resentment towards my grandmother – it was something anyone who ever spent more than a few minutes with her knew all about. So maybe he played on that to manipulate her into doing what he wanted. It isn't hard to believe that my mother – who was never someone to think things through and imagine what might be involved in the long term – would have agreed readily once the idea was planted in her head. Taking us away from my grandmother must have seemed like the perfect opportunity to get back at her and to vent some of her anger and hostility towards her family. What it might mean to my brother and me, however, was something that wouldn't have even crossed her mind, and certainly wouldn't have changed it if it had.

What was much more difficult to understand was what my mother could possibly see to attract her in Carl. He was in his fifties, with dirty-looking grey hair, uneven, nicotine-stained teeth and yellowish-grey skin that seemed at some time to have stretched until it was several sizes too large for his body. His arms and neck were completely covered in tattoos, and he wore thick glasses that magnified the permanently cold expression in his bloodshot eyes. He was very unattractive – in a grimy, creepy way – with his sallow skin, wispy hair, which was badly cut and too long, and the dark shadow of stubble that always covered his chin.

That first night when we arrived at his miserable flat, he must have thought he'd won the lottery. Somehow, he'd managed to get himself a young, pretty girlfriend who'd brought with her – most importantly of all to Carl, as it turned out – her vulnerable six-year-old daughter. And not only did his new girlfriend share his love of drinking, she was also usually too drunk to notice what was going on around her and too indifferent and self-engrossed even to think about trying to protect her children.

When we arrived at Carl's place, he opened a door off a dirty, dimly lit passageway and, without even looking at us, told Chris and me, 'That's your room. Go to bed.' My mother didn't come into the bedroom with us or try to reassure us that everything was going to be all right. She simply pushed at the door with her foot, nodded towards the narrow single bed in what was just a small, dingy box room, and told us we'd have to sleep head to toe. Then, giggling and having already forgotten we even existed, she followed Carl into what I assumed was his bedroom and shut the door.

Chris and I stood in the middle of the bare, cold little room and looked at each other. Then, trying not to cry, we climbed into the narrow, damp-smelling bed, fully clothed. Chris fell asleep as soon as his head hit the pillow but, although I was exhausted, I felt too uneasy and frightened to sleep. So I lay there on my back in the dark, tears dripping through my hair and on to the dirty sheet, and thought about my grandmother.

I didn't even know where we were. Sitting in the back of Carl's car on the way to our new home, I'd looked out of the window, searching for a familiar landmark that might help to orientate me. But I only knew a few of the streets around my grandparents' house, and I was already lost by the time we'd walked to the house of the man who let us use his phone. So I hadn't recognised anything as we sped through the dark, empty streets in Carl's car, and I knew that, even if I did manage to phone my grand-mother at some time, I wouldn't be able to tell her where we were. And if she didn't know where we were, she couldn't come and find us, which meant I might never see her again.

I tried to stifle the sob that rose up from the pit of my stomach, and at that moment the door of the box room was pushed open just far enough to allow a thin shaft of light to fall across my brother's face where he lay at the foot of the bed. I shut my eyes. Much as I might be longing for someone to comfort me, I wasn't going to give my mother the satisfaction of thinking I'd ever forgive her for dragging me from my grandparents' house in the middle of the night, and for taking me away from everyone and everything I loved.

I could smell the stale odour of cigarette smoke and alcohol that surrounded my mother wherever she went. But she didn't seem to be coming into the room, so I opened one eye just far enough to be able to make out the outline of her body through my eyelashes. And then I realised that the figure standing in the doorway was not my mother, but Carl. I quickly shut my eye again and my heart began to race as Carl staggered into the room and bumped against the side of the bed.

A moment later, I felt his hand moving under the bedclothes. I wanted to turn on my side so that I was facing away from him, but instead I lay perfectly still, as he touched my legs and then suddenly pushed his rough-skinned fingers inside my knickers. I was shocked, and terrified that he'd hear the thumping of my heart and know I wasn't really asleep. He continued to touch me for what seemed like an eternity, although in reality it was probably only a few seconds. Then he withdrew his hand and left the room, shutting out the light as he closed the door silently behind him.

My brother hadn't stirred in his sleep, and I lay there feeling very alone and trying to understand what had just happened. I was used to living with my mother's erratic, often inexplicable behaviour, but what Carl had just done seemed odd, even by my mother's standards. The room had a musty, dirty-clothes sort of smell, which suggested it hadn't been used for some time, so I decided eventually that Carl, who was clearly drunk, had probably just remembered he'd left something in the bed and had been trying to find it without waking us up. It wasn't a very convincing explanation, but it was the only one I could come up with.

I could still hear in my head the sound of my grandmother's sobs and I could see the anguished, heartbroken expression that had been on her face as my mother dragged Chris and me down the garden path earlier that night. And before I fell into an exhausted, fitful sleep, I silently prayed that when my mother woke up in the morning she'd decide she didn't want us to live with her after all and she'd take us home.

But it soon became clear that the prayer I'd made the first night wasn't going to be answered: Carl's grim, cramped little flat was to be our new home, and all the happy days of living with our grandparents had come to an end.

My grandmother always used to tell me that you can't judge a book by its cover. The first time she said it, I didn't understand what she meant, and she'd explained that it was another way of saying that what people look like on the outside doesn't necessarily tell you what they're like on the inside. So you shouldn't decide whether or not you like someone based on their appearance; you have to wait until you get to know them. I wanted to please my grandmother, so it was advice I always tried to follow. But there was something about Carl that made me think he looked the way he did *because* of what was inside him, which, whatever it was, wasn't something nice.

To other people, Carl presented himself as a hard-working, loving partner and stepfather. But when the front door closed, he was something else entirely. The real Carl was a drunken, disgusting human being, devoid of any empathy or compassion, who made me fear him and then used my fear to enable him to abuse me, physically, emotionally and sexually. As long as my mother was able to drink, she was happy – and oblivious to what was going on around her. So all Carl had to do was make sure she was never without a constant supply of alcohol, and then he was free to indulge whatever sick fantasy came into his mind.

Although my mother never mentioned my grandmother to us, other than to swear and complain about her, she must have made contact with her somehow. Because, after we'd been in the flat for a couple of days, she told us that in future she would take us to school on the train every morning and then my brother and I would walk to my grandparents' house at teatime, and stay there until she and Carl came to collect us after they finished work.

It had quickly become apparent that Carl didn't like my brother *or* me, and it must have been equally clear to Carl that I detested him. But even living with him and my mother in his horrible little flat might be bearable if I could see my grandmother every day. I was so excited at the prospect that I had to stop myself jumping up and down, because I knew better than to let my mother know how happy I was. I'd long ago learned not to tell her if something was important to me, because if I did, it meant that whenever she was in one of her moods or feeling mean, she could hurt me by taking away the one thing that might give me some pleasure. So I tried to appear indifferent, as though I didn't really care about seeing my grandparents, and I hoped my mother couldn't tell that my heart was doing cartwheels in my chest.

After lunch on the first day back at school, I hardly took my eyes off the large, oak-framed clock above the blackboard. The afternoon seemed to drag on for ever, but finally the last lesson of the day came to an end and I grabbed my little bag off the peg in the cloakroom and ran to the school gate. Then I stood there, kicking the wire netting that surrounded the playground, and waited impatiently until my brother almost flew out of the building, grasped my hand without a word and tried to keep up as I set off along the pavement as fast as my legs would carry me.

Rounding the corner of the street where my grandparents lived, we could see my grandmother waiting for us at the open front door. It had only been a few days since we'd last seen her – since the night when our mother had snatched us from the house – but it seemed like a lifetime. As we ran up the garden path, she squatted down and opened her arms and we almost knocked her over in our eagerness to feel them close around us.

Life soon settled into an uneasy but more or less regular pattern. I knew that, however miserable the days might be, for five out of seven of them every week I would spend at least a couple of hours with my grandparents, and sometimes with my aunts and uncles too. Saturdays and Sundays were the worst days. But we hadn't been living with Carl for very long when my mother started having an affair with another man she'd met at a pub. Almost every weekend after that, while Carl was out drinking with his mates, we'd trail after her reluctantly to her weekend-boyfriend's house, where we'd sit alone in the living room for hours on end, watching television, while they went upstairs and shut the bedroom door.

Eventually, she'd come tearing down the stairs again, shouting at us, 'Out! Out! Get moving for God's sake,' as though *we* had kept *her* waiting, rather than the other way round. Then she'd usher us out into the street, and we'd trot along behind her as she almost ran to my grandparents' house, where Carl would soon be arriving to collect us. She swore us to secrecy, making us promise again and again that if Carl asked, we'd say we'd been at our grandparents' house all day. We were used to keeping secrets, and we knew what would happen if we upset our mother. And although the weekends were almost unbearably boring, at least we hadn't been left alone with Carl, and I felt a small sense of satisfaction because I knew something he didn't.

One Saturday afternoon, when my grandparents were away for the weekend and Carl had arrived at their house to pick us up, he and my mother went into the living room to watch television and drink. They left the door slightly ajar, so that they could hear if Chris and I misbehaved in any way, and Carl told us to stay out of the room. Then he dragged an armchair across the carpet, positioned it so that it blocked the doorway, and sat down with his can of beer.

I was furious. It was one thing for my mother to tell me what to do, but how dare Carl think he could order me around in *my* grandparents' house?

Chris and I crept silently along the hallway and flattened ourselves against the wall beside the living-room door. Carl had already been drunk when he arrived at the house, and it wasn't long before he fell asleep. Just the top of his head was visible above the back of the chair, and I could see that if the door were to be pushed hard enough, it would hit him.

I nudged my brother, pointed at Carl's head and whispered, 'Go on, I dare you.' Then we both started to giggle, and almost fell over each other in our haste to get away from the open doorway before we burst into laughter.

When we were safely in the kitchen, I hissed at Chris again, 'I dare you. Just push the door, once, really hard.'

'No! I dare *you*,' he answered, pushing me ahead of him back up the hallway towards the living room.

We stood together for a moment looking at Carl's thin grey hair, and then, suddenly, I grabbed the door handle with both hands and rammed it as hard as I could against the back of his head. There was a loud crack and Carl leapt out of his chair, clutching his head with both hands and swearing, as Chris and I ran back to the kitchen, frightened, but almost choking with laughter.

I know we must have paid for our prank, although I can't remember how. Whatever the price, though, it was worth it for the fleeting sensation of knowing that, if only in a small way, I'd got my own back on the man who was responsible for ending my happy life with my grandparents and for making every single day of my new life so miserable.

I loved spending time with my grandparents. In contrast to the life I lived with Carl and my mother, everything in their house was clean, comfortable and well ordered, and every day spent with them followed a pattern I could understand and that made me feel secure, loved and accepted. Gradually, however, it began to feel as though something had changed. My grandmother and my aunts didn't laugh any more, and on more than one occasion I'd been certain I'd heard my grandmother crying.

Then, one day, I was watching television in the living room at my grandparents' house when I decided to go into the kitchen to ask my grandmother for a drink. As I walked towards the open kitchen door, I heard my aunt say, 'She knows something's wrong. It isn't fair, Mum. She *needs* to be told the truth.'

I wondered what she was talking about and guessed it

was probably something to do with my mother – 'wrong' things usually were.

'I don't want her to know,' my grandmother answered, her voice breaking as though she was suppressing a sob. 'The poor child has enough problems to deal with.'

I realised at that point that they were talking about me, and I began to feel afraid. I'd already learned that there are some things in life that, once you know them, can't ever be un-known and can change everything. And some sixth sense told me that this was one of those things.

'Please, Mother.' My aunt was almost begging.

For a moment, neither of them said anything, and I stood, frozen to the spot, as I tried to decide which I wanted more – to know or not to know what they were talking about.

Then my grandmother sighed a deep, unhappy sigh and said, 'Well, you'll have to tell her. I simply can't do it.'

I heard the familiar creaking of wood as my aunt rose from one of the old kitchen chairs, which, as my grandmother constantly reminded my grandfather, needed to have their joints re-secured. I turned and fled back into the living room, where I threw myself on to the sofa. A few seconds later, my aunt came into the room and sat down beside me. I ran the damp palms of my hands along my skirt and looked up at her, as she put her arm around my shoulders and began to stroke my hair.

'I've got something to tell you, Anna,' my aunt said, in a hesitant, tired-sounding voice. 'You're going to have to be a big, brave girl. Can you do that for me, darling?'

I nodded, although what I really wanted to do was shout at her, 'Don't tell me! I don't want to know.'

'Granddad is very ill,' she continued, pausing for a moment and making a small noise as though she was clearing her throat. 'He can't go to work any more. So he and Grandma are going to have to sell this house and go and live somewhere they can be looked after.'

By the time the words had passed from my ears to my brain they seemed to have become all jumbled up, and I couldn't really understand what she was saying. But the heavy, sick feeling in my stomach told me that something really bad was about to happen, something far worse than any of the many bad things that had happened so far in my life. I began to pray that my aunt would say something that I could understand, something that would make me realise everything was going to carry on as normal and be all right. But she just kept stroking my hair and holding me.

'Does that mean Chris and me will have to live all the time with Mummy…?' I swallowed, unwilling to add the words 'and Carl'.

When I looked at my aunt, I could see the answer in her expression, and I burst into tears as my entire world fell apart. The hours I spent with my grandparents were the only good times in my life. No one else loved me, and there was no one else I could turn to when everything became so horrible. I didn't think I could bear it any longer. It was terrible that my grandfather was ill, and I think I could sense the fact that he might be going to die. But my grandfather's death was something I couldn't even begin to imagine, whereas living alone with my mother and Carl was something I could.

6

Beaten, abused and unloved

THE FACT THAT we were living with them full time meant that Carl and my mother were able to get a council house – which turned out to be an old, run-down, two-bedroom house that was due for demolition in a few months' time. Although it was only about five miles from where my grandparents lived, it might just as well have been a million miles away, because living there was like living in a completely different world.

The move meant that not only was I losing my family and friends, but I also had to leave my school. And, in exchange, I was going to live with two self-engrossed and dedicated alcoholics, one of whom was mentally unstable and the other an abusive pervert who cared nothing for me at all. During the previous two years, I'd begun to take for granted the warm, comfortable, well-furnished home I'd lived in with my grandparents. And it was only when I tried to come to terms with living in a damp, cold house with peeling paint and almost no furniture that I realised just how lucky I'd been. My mother refused to decorate the house or buy any carpets for it, and the only floor covering we did have was a stair carpet that was given to us by a neighbour who was about to throw it out but who felt sorry for us and gave it to my mother instead.

I felt deeply ashamed of where I lived and deeply ashamed of the people I lived with. I'd been happy to take friends home from school to my grandparents' house, which was just like the houses they all lived in – clean and nicely furnished, with rugs and carpets and painted walls. The fact that my friends didn't even notice any of those things, which seemed so wonderful to me, was a good thing, because it confirmed what I wanted so desperately to be true: that I was a 'normal' little girl, living in 'normal' surroundings, just like they were.

I knew, though, that even if I did make friends at my new school, I wouldn't be able to take them back to the horrible, dirty, dilapidated house that was my new home. I hated its bare, splintered floorboards; the little flakes of paint that often dropped from the walls; the sparse, shabby, uncomfortable bits of furniture, and the lack of heating, which meant that every room in the house was as cold as it was uncomfortable. And if potential new friends didn't run a mile when they saw where I lived, they'd certainly do so when Carl started leering at them from his armchair, where he'd be sitting in his stained vest, displaying his horrible tattoos, or when they saw my mother passed out drunk on the sofa or, even worse, loud and aggressive and still in the process of drinking herself into a stupor.

Probably the only positive thing about living in that house with my mother and Carl was sharing a bedroom with Chris, although even that didn't stop Carl's night-time visits, particularly as Chris and I no longer had to share a bed.

Carl would have had to have been someone very special to compensate me for being taken away from my contented life with my grandparents, although in reality I'd probably have eventually settled down happily with someone who was 'quite nice'. But there was absolutely nothing nice about Carl at all.

Every night, as soon as my brother was asleep and my mother had fallen into her usual alcohol-induced coma, Carl would come into our bedroom. Sometimes, I'd be awake, and my stomach would lurch as his dark shape appeared in the doorway, almost blocking out the light from the landing behind him. I'd feel physically sick, and I'd shut my eyes and lie completely still, praying silently that something would distract him and he'd go away again. But however much I prayed, he always shuffled into the room and stood beside my bed. Then he'd bend down and put his face close to mine, so that I had to hold my breath and try not to retch as the stale stench of alcohol and tobacco hit my nostrils. Looking back now, I realise he must have known I wasn't really asleep, because by the time he slid his hand under my quilt, snaking it across the bed and forcing it between my legs, my body would be rigid with tension.

After the first night we'd spent at his flat, I'd worn my knickers in bed, hoping it might stop him touching me. But it only took him a couple of days to come up with a reason why I wasn't allowed to wear knickers and night-clothes together, although I can't now remember what it was. I tried everything else I could think of to stop him – lying on my side facing away from the door or on my back with my legs tightly clenched – but he was strong, and I was just six years old, so I don't suppose he even noticed my pathetic attempts at resistance.

I didn't know what he was doing when he put his hand under the bedclothes and touched me, and I didn't know why he was doing it; I just knew I hated it. I'd sometimes try to imagine that I was in bed at my grandparents' house, snuggling down under the bedcovers, feeling warm and safe while I waited for my grandmother to come and say goodnight to me. But it was too much of a stretch for my imagination, because my bed had become the place where I felt most vulnerable and afraid – afraid of what Carl was going to do to me while I lay awake, and even more afraid of what he might do if I went to sleep.

I realise now that Carl was grooming me, testing me to see how far he could go before I'd tell someone what he was doing. He needn't have bothered, though, because I had no one to tell. The only person I trusted was my brother, who was far too young to understand, and I couldn't talk to my mother about anything at all. For the last two years, she'd been just a figure in the background of my life who I hardly knew. And, in any case, she was the last person in the world anyone would confide in, because although she was always insisting that my brother and I must keep *her* secrets, she was totally incapable – and uninterested in – keeping secrets for anyone else.

Living with my mother was like living with the Mad Hatter. Her moods could change in an instant, as though they were controlled by a switch that flicked randomly on and off. So I never knew how to behave around her. One minute I could be talking to her and we'd be getting on well, and then, in the middle of a sentence, she'd suddenly become inexplicably furious, dragging me to the floor and punching me or hitting me on the head repeatedly, screaming, 'You're nothing but a selfish fucking bitch. You can forget about having any dinner tonight.'

Although it happened often, it was always a total shock, and in some ways the inconsistency of her behaviour and her sudden, violent mood swings were almost worse than if she'd been constantly angry. Time after time, we'd be having a calm, ordinary conversation and I'd be lulled into thinking everything was all right and that perhaps she really did like me, just a little. And then – bang! She'd go crazy.

Almost worse than my fear on those occasions, however, was the feeling that I was stupid for having been naive enough to think she could change.

After we began to live with Carl, all the stability was lost from my life, and replaced by fear and confusion, until there was just one remaining certainty: there was absolutely no one and nothing I could rely on.

I couldn't talk to my grandparents about what was happening at home, because my mother had sworn me to secrecy. She and Carl warned us repeatedly not to tell anyone what went on in our house, and I was frightened that if I *did* say something, my mother would get into trouble, which was something I didn't want to happen, for her sake and for my own, because if people were cross with my mother, she'd be even more cross with me.

I learned to live with lies, deceits and secrets and, inevitably, became withdrawn and uncommunicative. I never knew what I *was* allowed to talk about, so it seemed safer to remain silent. Perhaps worst of all, though, was the feeling that I was tainted by secrets I didn't really understand, which meant that I was locked inside the miserable, nasty little world Carl and my mother had created for themselves – and, coincidentally, for Chris and me as well.

I'd shared secrets with people when I lived with my grandparents, but they were exciting secrets about presents that had to be kept hidden until someone's birthday or treats that were being planned as a surprise. Although I didn't understand the secrets I was being told to keep now, I knew they were completely different, and that they had to be kept, not because revealing them would spoil something nice, but because if other people knew about them, something very bad would happen.

The house we lived in was more than 100 years old. It didn't smell of polish and cooking like my grandparents' house, but of damp and decay, to which my mother and Carl soon added the stench of cigarettes and spilt alcohol. Its ancient wooden floorboards creaked even when no one was walking on them, and I was filled with terror at the thought that someone or something lurked unseen in its dark corners.

The toilet was downstairs, and I was too afraid to use it at night – sometimes because Chris and I were all alone in the house, and sometimes because we weren't and I knew that to get to it I'd have to pass the door to the living room, where my mother and Carl were lying drunk. My fear of all the dark corners in the house meant that on nights when I woke up needing to go to the toilet and knew I wouldn't be able to hold it in till morning, I'd often pee in the small, rusty, cast-iron fireplace in the sparsely furnished bedroom I shared with my brother. As a consequence, it wasn't long before a room that had looked as though nothing could ever be done to make it any worse began to stink of stale urine.

One night, I woke up needing to go to the toilet and lay in bed trying to decide what to do. The prospect of going downstairs in the dark was frightening enough, but it was winter, and I knew that the cold dampness of my bed was nothing compared to the freezing temperature in the rest of the house. Even if I wrapped myself in my coat, by the time I got back to the bedroom I'd be shivering so violently that I'd never get back to sleep again. On the other hand, though, if I had a pee in the fireplace, I ran the risk of Carl coming into the room and catching me alone and out of bed. Although I couldn't imagine what he might do in that situation, some instinct told me it would be worse than what he did already on his nightly visits to the bedroom.

I raised my head and looked over at my brother's bed. He was fast asleep, curled into a ball and lying so close to the edge of the mattress that he was only prevented from falling out by the sheet that was tucked in around him. Since we'd left our grandparents' house, he'd begun to have regular bed-wetting accidents, and I suddenly had a brilliant idea. He'd probably wee in his bed himself before morning, so no one would be any the wiser if I did it first. I slipped out of my bed, lifted one side of my brother's bedcovers and, without waking him, emptied my bladder on to his mattress.

It must have been only a few minutes later when the bedroom door was pushed open and Carl came into the room. He stood for a moment beside Chris's bed and I shut my eyes and prayed, until I felt his hand moving under my bedcovers, touching me between my legs. And then it stopped.

The stench of alcohol was almost overpowering as he leaned over me and hissed angrily, 'You're a filthy little bitch; a filthy, disgusting little bitch.' Then he left the room.

The next morning, he told my mother I'd pissed in my brother's bed during the night. He must have put his hand on the wet mattress when he leaned over Chris to see if he was asleep, and then, when he felt the wetness between my legs, he'd realised what I'd done. However, my mother thought the idea was ridiculous.

'Don't be bloody stupid,' she snapped at Carl. 'What the fuck would she do that for?'

'I *did* not,' I added quickly, trying to look suitably indignant.

Carl glared at me. For just one brief moment I'd got the upper hand, and he was furious. I was lying, but he realised that if he insisted, my mother might begin to wonder how he knew. So all he could do was mouth 'Filthy little bitch' at me behind her back and then talk to her about something else.

It was never safe to relax in our house, which meant that even when I appeared to be absorbed in doing something, there was always a part of me that was alert, watching and listening. Carl had lots of 'games' he liked to play, all of which sounded innocent enough to my mother or to anyone else who might have overheard them, but which in fact had nothing whatsoever to do with fun.

If Carl and I were alone in the living room – which I tried to avoid whenever possible – he'd sit me on his knee and say, 'Let's kiss like Eskimos.' Then he'd rub his nose against mine and put his tongue into my mouth. Or he'd come into the room sucking on a boiled sweet, which he'd insist I should take from him, again putting his tongue in my mouth and almost making me choke.

Sometimes, I'd be sitting on the stained, foul-smelling sofa in the living room, watching television, when I'd hear a sound. I'd turn quickly towards the door and see Carl standing just inside the room, leering at me with a humourless grin that seemed to show every single one of his disgusting, yellow teeth. A dull ache would spread across my forehead and every muscle in my body would tense as I leaned away from him in an almost involuntary movement that I knew annoyed him. But he'd just keep grinning and call, in a slow, sing-song voice like a child's, 'I'm going to get you.'

My heart would start to thump and I'd whisper, 'No…please,' wiping the sweat from my hands on to my skirt as I stood up and started edging towards the door.

Carl would ignore me and call again, 'Here I come.' But although his tone was jokey, his eyes would be fixed, cold and unblinking, on my face as I groped along the wall behind me for the door. Then, without turning my back on him, I'd suddenly make a dash for the hallway and stand there for a moment, with my mind frozen, as I tried to decide where to go. Should I dart into the kitchen, where the radio was blaring and where my mother would be swigging from a bottle? Or should I run upstairs and try to find somewhere to hide? It was a choice I never really needed to make, though, because there was no escape.

Carl would come into the hall, still laughing but with a nasty expression in his eyes, and say, loudly enough for my mother to hear above the racket she was making in the kitchen, 'I'm going to tickle you! You can't stop me.' Then he'd grab me and throw me to the floor, pinning me down with his knees and starting to tickle me.

Despite the fear that would be welling up inside me, threatening to choke me, I'd be unable to stop myself laughing – to begin with – until Carl put one hand over my mouth and nose and forced the other between my legs or down my top to pinch my nipples painfully between his fingers.

Staring into my frightened eyes, he'd shout, 'Submit! Do you submit? I won't release you until you say you submit.' But I couldn't say anything, because his hand would be covering my mouth.

Gradually, Carl's 'games' became even more aggressive and more like vicious sexual assaults, which left dark, ugly bruises on my skin and red soreness between my legs.

'All fathers do this to their daughters,' Carl would tell me, whispering so that my mother couldn't hear him and ignoring the fact that I was fighting for breath beneath the weight of the hand he was pressing over my mouth. 'I'm going to be the one to take your virginity.'

I didn't know what he meant, but the way he said it made it sound like something even more frightening and horrible than any of the 'games' he already forced me to play. I was a skinny, fragile little girl, just six years old, and I didn't have the strength to fight him off. And when he got bored of his game, or thought my mother might be about to step out of the kitchen into the hallway, and let go of me, my face would be flushed and I'd have to try to straighten my dishevelled clothes and act as though nothing had happened.

I wanted to tell Carl to stop. I wanted to kick him and shout and scream into his face. And I wanted to tell my mother what he was really doing to me whenever he pretended to be, what he called, horsing around. But my mother's reactions were unpredictable at the best of times, and some instinct told me I'd be wasting my breath, and that rather than taking my side against Carl, her violent, frightening anger would be directed towards me.

Another perverted 'game' Carl liked to play involved bending me over his knee and spanking my bare bottom. First, though, he'd send my brother out of the room, telling him he could listen outside the door while I received my punishment for having been naughty in some way he never bothered to explain. Chris thought it was hilarious. But for me it was yet another painful humiliation because, in reality, the purpose of the spanking was almost never to punish me for something I'd done wrong. It was just another way for Carl to indulge his desire for sick gratification.

Every time Carl abused me, he told me afterwards that he loved me and he'd insist on my saying I loved him, too. Until we went to live with Carl, I thought I knew what love was – it was the feeling I had whenever I thought about my grandparents – but I certainly didn't feel that way towards him. In fact, I knew I didn't love him. I hated him. So I couldn't understand why he wanted me to say it, particularly because I knew he hated me, too. He often told both me and Chris, 'I hate you, you fucking little bastards.' And I was sure no one who loved me would do so many things to hurt me.

So I stubbornly refused to say what he wanted me to say. Then he'd get angry and upset and he'd ask me over and over again, 'Do you love me?' Until, finally, just to make him leave me alone, I'd grunt 'Yes'. But even that wasn't enough; before he gave up and left me alone I had to say 'I love you, Carl' at least a couple of times. It always seemed odd to me that even though he knew I'd only said it because he'd forced me to, it still made him happy. I decided it must be just one more of the many unpleasant, inexplicable things I was finding out about Carl, although maybe it wasn't my love he wanted so much as the satisfaction of knowing he could control me and that he could do something horrible to me and then force me to say I loved him.

The only time Carl was ever 'nice' to me was when he was sexually abusing me. And in some ways that was one of the worst aspects of what he did to me, because it caused so much confusion in my mind that later it quite literally nearly killed me.

Children's brains are naturally wired up to respond to

approval. Mostly, they learn to behave in certain ways because when they do, people praise them. If they're lucky, they're brought up by people like my grandparents, who teach them how to fit comfortably into society. But what my mother and Carl were doing was scrambling all the connections that had been made in my brain and making me uncertain about every single thing I'd ever thought was true.

I don't know whether Carl was trying to make me believe that 'loving' him was the same thing as having a sexual relationship with him, so that he could convince me that that's what I really wanted. Or perhaps in his own sick, depraved mind he thought I *did* love him, and that I wanted him to abuse me. In the end, though, all he achieved by what he did to me was to make it impossible for me to tell anyone I love them; even now, I struggle to say those words, and when I do, they just sound hollow and without any real meaning.

Carl hated me leaving the house. He said it was because he was afraid some other man would 'try it on' with me, and he warned me repeatedly that he was never going to allow me to have a boyfriend. I was six years old, but in his warped, evil mind he obviously believed that all men lusted after little girls, just like he did, and that I was every man's sexual fantasy. To keep me at home, he'd tell me frightening stories about how some man would grab me in the street if I went out alone, and then take me to the park or into the woods and push sticks up inside my body. Because of his stories, I started having terrifying nightmares that continued for years and that made me afraid to fall asleep at night, and I was soon too scared even to venture as far as the end of the garden on my own. And as I became more frightened, I became increasingly withdrawn and unable to communicate with anyone.

I don't think my mother had any idea what Carl was doing to me. She had a whole list of things she warned me repeatedly not to talk about to anyone. It was a list that was constantly expanding and at the top of it was the drinking that took place in the house. She told me that anything I saw or heard that had anything at all to do with drinking must be kept secret from her family, because otherwise they'd 'interfere'. So when Carl kept telling me 'What we do together must be a secret that you never tell to anyone', it didn't seem strange; it was just one more thing I had to keep to myself.

When anyone questioned me about my life at home or asked if my mother was still drinking, I'd always swear that everything was fine and that she never touched a drop of alcohol. And it wasn't just fear of her reaction that made me lie. I had a strong (and totally undeserved) sense of loyalty towards my mother. I knew there was a lot of conflict between her and the rest of her family, and I thought that if she got into trouble, she might have to go back to hospital, which I knew she would have hated.

One day, we were invited to a family christening – on the condition that my mother didn't drink while we were there. During the party, which was held at my aunt's house after the ceremony in the church, my mother kept disappearing, and when my grandmother asked me to go into the kitchen to fetch a clean plate after someone had dropped theirs upside down on the carpet, I found her there. She'd been sneaking in and swigging out of the bottles of wine that were waiting to be served to the guests, and when I saw what she was doing she swore me to secrecy, grasping my arm tightly and hissing threats and warnings into my ear.

Later, after my mother had accidentally pushed a cork into a wine bottle and it became clear that she was helping herself in the kitchen, one of my aunts confronted her in front of everyone. My mother screamed at my aunt that she was 'a fucking liar', and a few minutes later Chris and I were running along behind her as she strode down the street, pausing occasionally to shout abuse and make wildly elaborate V signs in the direction of my aunt's house.

When I'd lived with my grandparents, I'd always been cheerful and open – so chatty, in fact, that it had often been difficult to shut me up! But after a few months with my mother and Carl, having to keep so many secrets and never being sure what I was allowed to talk about, I'd become guarded when anyone spoke to me. I must have seemed surly and unresponsive, and my aunts and uncles began to get irritated with me, because if any of them asked me a question, I'd look up at the sky, trying to give my brain time to process all the possible outcomes if I answered it, and then I'd shrug and say, 'I dunno.'

I simply couldn't unscramble all the don'ts that were whirling around in my head. So it seemed best to refuse to answer even the most straightforward question, and never to voice an opinion about anything. My grandparents, aunts and uncles must have thought my mother was turning me against them. But the truth was that although I could see the impatience in their faces and longed to be able to talk to them, there didn't seem to be any alternative other than to bottle everything up inside me and say nothing. I hated myself for doing it, though, not least because I began to feel as though they didn't love me any more. And if my grandparents, aunts and uncles didn't love me, my mother, father and Carl must be right after all, and I *was* worthless.

I sometimes used to think that my mother's family should have known something was wrong. In just a few months I'd transformed from being an outgoing, popular and happy little girl into a shifty and unfriendly child. But what Carl was doing to me would have been completely beyond their imagination and understanding. And, of course, they were preoccupied by my grandfather's serious illness and by selling my grandparents' house.

So, as the days, weeks and months passed, my mother continued to drink, Carl continued to abuse me, and I grew increasingly unwilling to open my mouth in public.

I was still just six years old the first time Carl had penetrative sex with me. It happened one Sunday morning – at a time when, just a few months previously, I'd have been waking up in my warm, comfortable bed at my grandparents' house before getting ready to go to Sunday school. On this particular morning, though, I woke up with excruciating earache, crawled out of the bed in the cold, cheerless room I shared with my brother and crept, sobbing, into the bedroom my mother shared with Carl.

Although it was clear that I was in a great deal of pain, my mother and Carl were annoyed at being woken up. Eventually, though, even my mother realised she had to do something to help me and she got up, threw on some clothes and said she was going out to see if the local shop was open so that she could buy me some medicine.

'Anna can stay here with me,' Carl told her, his voice full of a concern he'd certainly never felt for me before. 'She can just lie here with me in bed.' He turned to look at me and when I saw the spiteful expression in his narrowed eyes, I realised his caring words were just a pretence. 'I can't manage with Chris too, though. You'll have to wake him up and take him with you.'

At first, my mother argued, but Carl was insistent, and in the end she helped me climb into bed beside him and then dragged poor Chris to the shops with her.

As soon as they'd gone, I tried to get as far away across the bed from Carl as possible, turning my back on him and curling up into ball. He waited until he heard the sound of the front door slamming shut and then he began to touch me. I was crying as I tried to wriggle away from him and shake his hands off my body. But he just kept shifting his position in the bed behind me and touching me again, scratching my skin with his rough, calloused fingers. Then he pressed my lower thigh down on to the bed and I felt a sharp flash of pain as he forced his penis inside me. I didn't know what he was doing, but the throbbing ache in my ear was making my head feel as though it was about to explode and, as I screamed 'Get off me!', I kicked out at him without even thinking about the consequences.

He grabbed hold of my arm and almost lifted my whole body off the bed as he twisted me round until I was facing him. I shut my eyes and tried to turn my head away.

'There's nothing wrong with your ear,' he sneered. 'You're a fucking liar. You just want attention. Well, that's okay, because I'm going to give you some.'

I didn't know what he meant or what he was going to do to me, but I did realise that the fact that I was in agony was a matter of complete indifference to him. Still gripping my arm, he pushed me across the bed and on to my side, so that I was once again facing away from him, and I felt his penis rubbing against my bottom. I struggled and cried out, and at that moment I heard the sound of footsteps on the stairs and my mother's voice calling, 'We're back.'

Carl leapt out of bed as though he'd been stung. Then he glared at me with an expression of pure hatred, hissed 'Fucking bitch!' and walked out of the bedroom.

As well as sexually abusing me, Carl physically abused Chris and me. The first time he took off his belt and beat us was when I tried to do something to put an end to his nightly visits to our bedroom. I'd been thinking about it for some time, and then one night, after we'd gone to bed and were supposed to be asleep, I persuaded Chris to help me push my bed against the wall underneath the window and then push his bed up against the other side of it. The beds were heavy, and trying to manoeuvre them into position was difficult for two small children. But it was worth the effort, because when we jumped back into them again, it was clear that the only way anyone could get to my bed was by climbing across my brother's.

My mother and Carl were downstairs watching television, and although we tried to be quiet, it was impossible to prevent the beds making loud scraping noises as we dragged them across the bare floorboards. My mother was always reluctant to leave Carl alone with the bottle of booze they shared every night, and it took a lot to get her out of her chair once she'd settled for the evening. But we'd only been back in bed for a few seconds when Carl pounded up the stairs, flung open the bedroom door and started screaming obscenities at us. He was still screaming when he pulled off his belt and began to beat us with it, cutting into our tender skin until it bled. Then he slammed the bedroom door and stomped back down the stairs, leaving Chris and me sobbing hysterically.

I felt especially bad for my brother, because I had been responsible for involving him in moving the beds, which I'd wanted to do for reasons he didn't even understand. I was still cuddling him when we heard my mother's footsteps coming slowly up the stairs.

'Don't let her see us crying,' I whispered to Chris. 'Pretend it didn't hurt.'

Although my mother often flew into rages, punching and kicking us, her attacks were vicious but unpremeditated and random. She had never beaten us as a cold, deliberate punishment, and she seemed to feel guilty for what had just happened.

'Are you okay?' she asked in a quiet, child-like voice.

'It didn't hurt us anyway,' I snapped at her.

'It wasn't supposed to hurt you,' she said, meekly. 'Carl was just cross because you were misbehaving when you were supposed to be going to sleep.'

I turned away from her and didn't answer. Unreasonably perhaps, because she didn't know what her disgusting paedophile boyfriend was doing to me, but I was furious with her. I'd been belted for the crime of trying to protect myself, and my brother had been belted for helping me, when the only reason I'd done what I did was because *she* didn't protect us herself.

'Well…um, go to sleep now,' she finished lamely. Then she closed the door and Chris and I cuddled each other as we cried ourselves to sleep.

The next morning, no one mentioned what had happened; Carl just insisted we must put our beds back the way they used to be. And by the time night fell again and he crept into our bedroom, his access to me was once more unimpeded.

7

Bad becomes worse

IF ANYONE HAD offered me three wishes, one of them would have been to move out of the house we were living in. So maybe people are right when they say 'Be careful what you wish for', because the place the council eventually moved us into, just before my seventh birthday, was even worse.

Our new home was a wooden, pre-fabricated house on a no-hope, run-down estate where it seemed that the council had corralled together all the most determinedly antisocial, dysfunctional families in the county. The flat-packed houses had originally been built to provide temporary accommodation, but somehow, over the years, they'd become permanent, although by the time we moved in, they looked as though they were finally coming to the end of their over-extended lifespan.

Each house was identical to its neighbours, and beside each one was an ugly, pebble-dashed garage with solid metal doors painted a depressing grey colour. Few of the gardens had anything in them other than old cars and rusting household items. But it was only when you went inside the houses that you realised just how miserable they really were. Their walls were made of plasterboard, which, in our house at least, was dented and full of holes that had been made over the years by fists raised in anger and frustration. The house's one advantage over our previous house was that it had an extra, third, bedroom, although, in fact, sleeping in a room on my own was the last thing in the world I wanted to do.

The estate had a deservedly bad reputation, and living there was like living with a constant reminder that you'd reached the end of the road. There was nowhere to go but up, and it was clear to all the residents that up was somewhere they most definitely weren't heading. No one on that estate expected anything good to happen to them, and no one had any expectations that their children might live lives that were any different from their own. Everyone knew everyone else's business and almost everyone was receiving social security. It was as though *having* anything was viewed as some sort of treachery to the group, because if anyone ever managed to wangle something extra for themselves, they'd immediately be reported by their neighbours to social services or the police.

Just as she'd done at our last house, my mother refused to buy carpets or to spend any money on anything that might make it seem less like a hovel that even the most desperate squatter would reject – although God knows what miracle of homemaking would have been needed to achieve that end. Her excuse was that she wasn't going to waste good money improving a council house that wasn't hers. She always liked to feel she'd outsmarted someone, and the fact that in doing so she was making life even more miserable and uncomfortable for all of us didn't seem to matter.

Apparently, we couldn't afford heating either. My mother resolutely refused to turn it on during even the coldest weeks of the year, and as the outer walls of the house were made of plasterboard covered by a layer of wood cladding, it was always absolutely freezing. We kept our coats on in the house for most of the winter, and when my brother and I came home from school, we'd sit on the sofa in the soulless little living room and wrap ourselves in blankets to try to keep out the bitter cold. The only bright side of living in that house when the temperature was below zero was that the water that normally ran down the walls and collected in puddles on the windowsills turned to ice, and for a while you couldn't smell the damp or the stench of the black mould that formed a permanent coating over the peeling paint on the window frames.

I didn't understand how everyone except us seemed to be able to afford to heat their homes, particularly because, unlike many of the adults on the estate, my mother and Carl both had jobs. And I didn't understand why we were penniless, as they claimed, and, if we were, how they could afford to buy a bottle of Bacardi to share between them every single weekday evening, and then spend every weekend drinking in pubs.

Apart from the horrible house, one of the worst things about moving to the estate was that I had to leave the school I loved and go to the local primary school. I'd been surprised by how easily I fitted in and made friends at my last school, when I was living with my grandparents, but at the new one, things were very different. As soon as we moved into the new house, all the kids on the estate came sniffing round, and they seemed to take an instant dislike to me and Chris. Almost from day one, they bullied us, shouting abuse at us and calling us snobs because of the way we spoke and dressed – in the clothes our grandparents had bought for us. I was thin and small for my age, with blonde hair and blue eyes, and maybe I looked timid, like someone who could be easily bullied. But they soon discovered they'd made a serious mistake, because I don't suppose any of the other kids had as much unhappiness and pent-up anger inside them as I did, and it was just waiting for an excuse to burst out.

The other children's nastiness and intense dislike of me meant nothing, because there was no one on earth who hated me more than I hated myself. So I had nothing to lose, and I became fearless, lashing out at anyone who confronted me, and fighting viciously with anyone who tried to take me on. And I soon proved I was a damn sight tougher than any of them. As a child in that sort of environment, you either learn to survive or you go under, and I was a quick learner. Before long, I'd earned a reputation for being hard. All the children on the estate were afraid of me, and all the parents warned their kids to keep away from me. But I wasn't tough enough to stop Carl abusing me.

After the move, my mother decided that my brother and I should take Carl's surname, so that everyone would think he was our father, and also so that our real father wouldn't be able to find us if he ever came looking for us – which seemed unlikely. But Carl *wasn't* my father, and although my parents were already divorced by the time we moved in with him, my mother didn't marry him, so he wasn't even my stepfather, and I resented having to change my name. Even worse than having Carl's surname, however, was the fact that we were expected to lie by telling anyone who asked that he was our father, which I refused to do. I hated him, and I made it clear to my teachers and to any new friends I made that he wasn't my dad, claiming that I didn't know who my real dad was.

On the Friday before Father's Day, we made cards and little presents at school, but I was determined not to make anything for Carl. The first year I was at the school I went to when we moved to the estate, I woke up on the Friday morning and managed to persuade my mother I was ill. For some reason, though, that didn't work the following year, and when we trooped back into the classroom after lunch, my teacher announced in front of all the other kids that I was excused from the card and present making.

Waving her hand dismissively, she told me, 'Go to the back of the classroom and tidy the books on the bookshelves.'

I felt my face flush with humiliation. My fatherless state was something I very rarely talked about and, when I did, it was only to my friends. But now everyone in the class knew. I'd been singled out as a child who had no father and I felt as though I was the only one, although in reality that can't have been the case, because there were lots of single-parent (almost exclusively mother-only) families on the estate. Perhaps it was just that the other kids preferred to pretend. Or perhaps they did all have some sort of father-figure in their lives who they didn't feel the need to dissociate themselves from.

Although I felt as though I was going to burst into tears and I wished the earth would open and swallow me up, I managed to put on my 'I don't care' expression as I strode, head held high, towards the back of the classroom.

I was passing the table where my best friend, Louise, was sitting when she raised her hand and said, 'I don't want to make a card either, Miss. Can I help Anna?'

'But, Louise, surely you want to make something to give to your father on Sunday?' The teacher sounded surprised and disapproving.

'No, I don't,' Louise snapped back at her.

'Well, I suppose…If you're certain…' Miss Harris didn't sound convinced. But Louise was already on her feet and walking towards the back of the classroom, where she nudged me with her elbow and gave me a huge grin.

'Why did you do that?' I whispered to her.

'Because I wanted to be with you,' she answered, as if that was explanation enough.

If I hadn't already grown wary of touching people or of being touched by them, I'd have given her a hug. She probably never realised how grateful I was to her for what she did that day. I knew she really wanted to make something for her father, but she could see beneath my bravado and she chose instead to sort bookshelves with me so that I didn't have to spend the afternoon alone at the back of the classroom with only my humiliation to keep me company.

The one light at the end of the long, dark, hopeless tunnel in which we lived was the fact that my mother always insisted on a member of her family coming to collect my brother and me on the last day of every term, and not returning us until the day before the new term started. At the beginning of each school holiday, she'd send us off with a list of things she expected my aunts and uncles to buy for us, which always included new school shoes, coats and various other items of clothing. And they bought us every single thing on the list, as well as looking after us and allowing us to be children again for a few precious weeks.

I don't think my aunts and uncles really understood what they were doing for us. Going on those holidays was like taking a deep lungful of fresh air after holding my breath for weeks on end in a stifling, toxic environment. That may sound dramatic, but I was sure that, without those breaks away from my mother's crazy moods and the unrelenting misery of Carl's abuse, I'd have suffocated and died.

When we got home again at the end of the holiday, there'd be no warm welcome for us, no specially prepared meal and questions about what we'd been doing, like there always were when we arrived at our aunts' and uncles' houses. I'd go straight up to my bedroom to be alone while I tried to come to terms with the prospect of the miserable, empty weeks that stretched ahead of me. After a few minutes, my mother would come bursting in, banging open the door so that it swung back against the flimsy bedroom wall, and screaming, 'What the fuck's the matter with you, you stuck-up little bitch? Why don't you fuck off back to your aunt's if you hate it so much here?'

Then I'd feel guilty as well as depressed, because the truth was that I'd have given *anything* to 'fuck off back to my aunt's'. I'd say nothing, though, and my mother would keep on shouting until she'd made me cry. So, in some ways, going to stay with my aunts and uncles made me feel even more wretched than usual, because although those holidays gave me an insight into what family life should and could be like, they were such an extraordinary contrast to the life I was living at home that coming back was almost harder to bear than never leaving.

Every term, I'd bottle up all my unhappiness inside me, only occasionally releasing some of the built-up pressure by fighting with any of the local kids who made the mistake of trying to bully me. I wasn't good at talking about how I felt, and there was no one to talk to anyway, so it wasn't long before anger became my only form of expression. I felt imprisoned, too, by my mother's rage and by her hostility towards me. Even when I was physically removed from her and staying with my aunts and uncles, it was as though she and Carl had spread their poison into every corner of my childhood, killing my innocence and destroying any chance I might otherwise have had to be a happy little girl.

My mother and Carl never showed any affection towards me. Neither of them ever spoke to me kindly, and they never tried to comfort me when I was sad; they only sneered and jeered at me. So, whenever I had any sort of problem, I had no one to turn to for advice.

One Sunday morning, when I was ten years old, I looked in the mirror in the bathroom and saw that my face was covered in spots. I didn't know what had caused them, but I was mortified. Carl was always accusing me of being 'a dirty fucking shite', and it seemed he was right.

I dreaded the thought of anyone seeing my face. But I couldn't hide upstairs for ever, and when I eventually went down for breakfast, Carl immediately began taunting me. At first he laughed, and then he pretended to be disgusted, telling my brother not to touch me in case he caught some terrible disease from someone who didn't wash properly. I was determined not to give him the satisfaction of seeing me burst into tears, although it took all my effort not to cry.

I was sure that everyone who saw the spots would be as revolted as Carl was. So, that night, I sat in the bath,

rubbed the bristles of the scrubbing brush into the soap
and dragged it backwards and forwards across my nose,
cheeks, chin and forehead until the skin was raw and
bleeding. By the next morning, the grazes had already
started to heal and my face was covered in dozens of thin
scabs. I was shocked when I saw it in the mirror, but at least
I'd got rid of the spots. There was nothing more I could do,
except try to prepare myself for the teasing and cruel
comments I knew I'd be subjected to when I got to school.

As we walked to school together, I kept asking my
brother, 'Will everyone notice them? What will they
think they are?' He tried to reassure me, but I could tell
from the way he hesitated before he answered and from
the expression of anxious pity in his eyes that they were as
bad as I thought they were.

In the event, however, few of the kids at school were
given the opportunity to torment me, because as I opened
the door to my classroom, my teacher looked up and
shrieked in horror, 'Good Lord, Anna!' Then she almost
ran across the room towards me, flapping her hands as
though to shoo me away and shouting, 'What on earth's
the matter with your face?'

She stopped abruptly a few feet away from me and held
up her hand like a traffic policeman stopping cars.
Behind her, children were sniggering and making sounds
of disgust, but she did nothing to quieten them.

'I…I don't know, Miss,' I muttered, hanging my head so that my hair fell over my face.

'I know what it is!' she screeched suddenly. 'It's impetigo! It's highly contagious. You must go home immediately, and you must not return until every single scab has healed completely. Go on.' She waved both hands at me again impatiently. 'Go to the office and tell the secretary that I've said you must go home.'

That night, Carl seemed delighted to have the opportunity to torment me even more than usual. Teasing me was part of his regular evening's entertainment, and he'd encourage my mother and brother to join in until I was sobbing hysterically. Then they'd all pretend to comfort me. Every time I'd believe they were really sorry, but as soon as my sobs had been reduced to the occasional hiccup or sniff, Carl would start again, sneering at me and mimicking my crying, contemptuous of my pathetic willingness to believe that, this time, they didn't mean it.

Carl had lots of reasons to tease me, and as he sat in the living room drinking every night, he'd amuse himself by picking away at the tattered remains of my self-esteem. He'd make up rhymes about my skinny legs or about the twitch I'd developed after all the years of anxious wariness and of being subjected to sudden, unexpected attacks by my mother.

Perhaps Carl's greatest skill, though, lay in his ability to manipulate my mother. Although I found it impossible to guess how she might react in any given situation, he knew just what buttons to press to get what he wanted from her.

For example, not long after we'd moved into the prefab house, Carl contacted his daughter, who was the same age as my mother. For years, she'd refused to have anything to do with him, but he managed to persuade her to visit for the weekend by saying he wanted her to meet his new family. In fact, though, my mother, brother and I were going to be away on that particular weekend, because we'd been invited to stay with one of my aunts for a family get-together – as Carl was well aware.

When Carl told my mother about his daughter's planned visit, she was determined to meet her. She tried to make him change the arrangement to another weekend, but he told her that his daughter had refused to come if my mother was going to be there. Instantly, my mother hated her, and over the next few days, she'd work herself into a rage whenever she was drunk and start shouting, 'That fucking bitch! Who the hell does she think she is?'

The weekend we were away, Carl's daughter travelled halfway across the country expecting to meet us, and arrived to find that her father had deceived her and was anticipating a weekend of having sex with her. But he hadn't taken into account the fact that she was no longer the frightened little girl he used to abuse, and as soon as she realised there was no one else in the house, she picked up her bag, opened the front door and left.

It must have been almost immediately after that when Carl phoned my mother, whingeing and whining and pleading with her to come home. He told her his daughter had refused to stay because she said the house was a dump and there was no food in the larder. It was an explanation he'd made up because he knew it would make my mother over-react – as she did about almost anything and everything – and it clearly worked, because, for ages afterwards, her drunken tirades often included reference to 'that stuck-up bitch, Carl's fucking daughter'.

My mother couldn't think rationally at the best of times, and her favourite stories seemed to be the ones that allowed her to rant and rave. But, even at the age of seven, I found it hard to believe that someone would travel miles to see the father they hadn't seen for years and then decide not to stay simply because there wasn't enough food in the house. It wasn't until years later, though, that I found out what had actually happened, and for a while I shared my mother's hatred of Carl's daughter – but for different reasons.

After suffering years of sexual abuse at Carl's hands, and knowing that his new family included a little girl of just seven years old, why didn't she try to do something to help me? If I thought today that a child was being abused – whether he or she was someone I knew or a total stranger – I'd shift heaven and earth to protect them. I can only guess that maybe Carl's daughter thought Carl's perverted sexual appetite was only related to her, and that any other child in his care would be safe from his abuse. I hope that's the case, because if she *did* suspect what was going on and chose to do nothing, I'd find that very hard to forgive.

There were so many disaffected families and so much antisocial behaviour on the estate that you'd have thought it virtually impossible for anyone to stand out as being worse than everyone else. But that was what my mother managed to achieve.

One of the first things she'd told me to do after we went to live there was to find the nearest doctor's surgery. As well as being an alcoholic, she abused prescription drugs, which she took in order to enhance the effects of the alcohol she drank. She claimed that the two together made her feel 'better', and it seemed she only had to ask a doctor for Valium, lithium or sleeping tablets and they were given to her. So, by her mid-twenties, she'd already developed a very high tolerance to both drugs and alcohol, although Chris and I still had to call out an ambulance on many occasions when we found her collapsed on the sofa, covered in her own vomit, and we couldn't wake her up. Sometimes she'd overdosed accidentally, and sometimes the weight of the depression she suffered from throughout her life had crushed her will to live.

The first time she met our new doctor on the estate was when she was drunk and had decided to walk up to the surgery in the early hours of one morning. When the doctor arrived for work a few hours later, he found her lying in a ditch at the side of the road. At first, he thought she was dead, and perhaps it was relief at discovering she wasn't that clouded his judgement long enough for him to agree to become her GP. It was a decision he must have lived to regret, as I don't believe anyone would have been willing to take on my mother as a patient if they'd known how much trouble she'd cause them.

Carl and my mother had a nightly ritual that never altered: every evening, they took two hand-cut crystal glasses out of the kitchen cupboard and opened a new bottle of Bacardi. They liked to drink out of expensive tumblers because they believed that it reflected the fact that they weren't just common drunkards; they were something special.

Once the Bacardi bottle was open, it would have taken a violent force of nature to make my mother leave her drink for any reason, because she was convinced that if she left the bottle unguarded for even a moment, Carl would take more than his share. Just the possibility that he might have had one more drink from it than she'd had was enough to spark a violent row. So she never came upstairs to tuck us in and say goodnight, which is what Carl was relying on when he took us up to bed each night.

8

Worse becomes wretched

ALMOST EVERY NIGHT, Carl would watch me while I got undressed. Then he'd hang around on the landing until Chris had gone to bed, before coming into my bedroom to abuse me.

He'd be holding a towel in one hand and a flannel rinsed out in hot water in the other, and he'd pull the covers back from my bed, lift up my nightdress, part my legs with his short, stumpy tattooed fingers and wash me. Then, as he dried me with the towel, he'd tell me how important it was for that part of my body to be washed particularly well, and I'd notice how his face grew older and uglier as he spoke. He'd ask me questions, too, about whether my friends ever discussed their fathers touching them. And when I told him they didn't, he called me a liar, assuring me that all fathers did exactly the same thing to their daughters.

At that time, and for a long time afterwards, when Carl did things to me that I hated, I had no idea I had the right to say 'No' – although perhaps that was just as well, because it would only have made him angry and violent towards me. I was too young and naive for it even to have crossed my mind that what he was doing might not be normal, and I used to wonder if my mother had asked him to wash me like that. It had never happened at my grandparents' house, but I just accepted it, as I accepted so many other unacceptable things, including being attacked and screamed at by my own mother.

Another thing I came to dread was Carl giving us our nightly bath. First, he'd run scalding hot water into the bathtub and then he'd watch impassively while we squirmed and cried out in pain as we tried to do what he told us and 'get into the fucking bath'. According to Carl, bathing in boiling hot water was the only way to make sure we were really clean, and once again I accepted what he said without question. I've never understood why he did it to us – whether it was just because he enjoyed feeling he had the power to make us do whatever he liked, or whether it was because he hated us so much he liked seeing us suffer. But whatever warped, perverted reasoning lay behind it, by the time we got out of the bath we'd feel sick and faint, and our skin would be so red and sore that Carl had to cover us in talcum powder so that our mother didn't notice and realise what he'd done.

Sometimes, he'd fill the bath with hot rather than scalding water, and then he'd take off his clothes and climb in with us. He acted as though it was fun, but I hated it. I hated knowing that he was sitting behind me where I couldn't see him, laughing at my brother over the top of my head and making fun of me. Sometimes, without any warning, he'd grab hold of me, wrap his arms tightly around my stomach and start trying to push his penis into my bottom. I'd be startled by the suddenness of his action and often by a searing flash of pain, and I'd be embarrassed because Chris was looking straight at me. I'd try to push Carl away with my elbows, but he'd just tighten his grip until I could hardly breathe, and then he'd let go of me abruptly, get to his feet and wrap a towel around his waist before leaving the bathroom.

Then, one day, I heard my mother telling Carl that Chris and I were old enough to start having baths on our own. I was so delighted I almost shouted out loud, but I wanted to hear what Carl was going to say, so I managed to stay quiet as I stood by the open living-room door and listened. He began to argue with my mother, and I could tell he was trying to sound reasonable and hide the annoyance I could detect in his voice. I smiled to myself at the thought that he was wasting his time, because when my mother made up her mind she rarely changed it. Carl, too, must have realised he wasn't going to convince her, and he soon began to talk about something else, although I knew that that wasn't the end of the matter. He was as devious and determined to get his own way as my mother was and, as I knew he would, he soon came up with an alternative plan.

One day, he announced that in future I was not to get out of the bath until he came to dry me. He claimed that it was because I got water everywhere and regularly soaked the entire bathroom. That wasn't true, but as my mother never came upstairs when we were getting ready for bed, she took Carl's word for it and, after that, I always had to call him when I'd finished my bath. I would stay in the cooling water for as long as I could, sometimes until I was shivering with cold, but eventually I'd have to shout through the open bathroom door and then sit listening to the sound of his feet thudding up the stairs towards me.

He'd make me stand in the bath while the water drained away, and then he'd wipe every inch of my body with a sponge before I was allowed to touch a towel or step out on to the bathmat. I hated him running his horrible hands all over me and I tried and tried to think of some way to outwit him. I'd never really thought of simply disobeying him, but, eventually, when I'd run out of any other ideas, I washed myself quickly one day and then jumped out of the bath, dried myself on a towel and ran into my bedroom.

When Carl came upstairs and realised I hadn't waited for him to sponge me dry, he flew into a terrible rage. Ripping the belt from his trousers, he lashed it repeatedly across my bare body, shouting, 'You fucking little bastard! You got the fucking place soaking.' I hadn't, but I knew there was no point trying to defend myself.

The best nights were those when Chris and I were left alone in the house while Carl and my mother went to the pub or a casino. We were used to being left to look after ourselves, and it wasn't until a friend of mine stayed over one night that I discovered other parents didn't leave their children home on their own while they went out.

My brother, my friend and I were sitting on the sofa together, watching a late-night horror film on TV, when my friend suddenly asked, 'Where's your mum?'

'She's at the pub,' I answered, snuggling further down under the blanket we'd spread across ourselves.

'Aren't you worried about her?' My friend sounded surprised.

'No. Why should I be worried about her?' Although I shrugged as though I wasn't concerned, what I really meant was 'no more than usual', because the truth was that I worried about my mother all the time.

'If my mum knew we were going to be here on our own, she wouldn't have let me stay,' my friend said, and then added in a thoughtful voice, 'I think we better not tell her.'

'Okay,' I agreed, storing away this new bit of information about what was normal in other families so that I could think about it later.

Although my mother didn't have a driving licence, she was often the one who drove home in the early hours of the morning after she and Carl had been to the pub, because despite the fact that she'd be almost too drunk to get up the stairs, Carl would be worse.

One night after they'd been out, I woke up with my heart thumping as Carl came crashing into my bedroom. My mother must have passed out downstairs as soon as they got home, because he obviously wasn't afraid of her hearing him. He stood in the doorway for a moment, one hand resting against the door as he tried to regain his balance, and then he staggered towards my bed. I could smell the familiar stench of cigarettes and drink as he leaned down towards me, dragged the covers on to the floor, and tried to force his hands between my thighs. He was being rougher than usual and he was hurting me. I twisted my hips to try to turn away from him. But he grabbed my legs and flipped me over on to my back, hissing, 'You love it, you dirty little bitch. Open your legs.' I kicked out at him and shouted 'Bugger off!' and then, ridiculously, was instantly terrified of getting into trouble for swearing at him.

He was so drunk he kept falling backwards against the cupboard behind him, and eventually he gave up and staggered out of my bedroom. And it was then that I realised that whenever my mother was in a drunken stupor – which was almost every night – Carl could do exactly what he liked to me, safe in the knowledge that she would never wake up and come to my defence.

After that night, I became convinced he was going to murder us all, and I'd lie in bed shaking as I listened to him downstairs, becoming louder and more aggressive with each drink. I was determined to stay awake. My heart would be pounding and my fists would be clenched so tightly that my fingernails left small, red, half-moon-shaped marks on the sweating palms of my hands. The worst thing of all, though, was the thought that when the time came and he made his move to try to kill us, I would be responsible for protecting my mother and brother.

Although I was always very frightened of Carl, I became more defiant towards him in some ways as I got older. I continued to refuse to call him Dad, and I tried not to speak to him at all unless I had to, and then I'd get his attention by shouting 'Oi!' It always made him furious. He'd accuse me of being rude to him and not appreciating him, and then – to my amazement – he'd have the nerve to whine to my mother that I didn't show him any respect.

I'd do everything I could think of to avoid being alone in the house with him. If ever I had to go home before my mother was there, I'd sit outside at the front, near the pavement, and wait for her – even if it was pouring with rain and pitch dark. If I was in the house when my mother went out and I had to stay there for some reason, I'd run silently up the stairs and hide in the wicker washing basket, which was in the cupboard in my mother's (and Carl's) bedroom. I was just small and skinny enough to fit inside, and I'd pull the dirty clothes over my head and close the lid. Then I'd wait there until my mother came home, holding my breath as I listened to Carl searching the house for me. Sometimes, he'd call my name angrily, and sometimes his tone would be cajoling and he'd promise he wasn't going to 'do' anything to me. He often opened the door of the cupboard where I was hiding, but he never found me, and each time I felt a thrill of satisfaction knowing that I'd outsmarted and frustrated him.

One day, I was in the front garden when my mother came out of the house with Chris and asked, 'Do you want to come with us? We're going to the shop.'

'No, I'll wait here till you get back,' I told her.

She shrugged and said, 'Okay. Please yourself,' and as she pushed Chris through the gate ahead of her, I heard him say, 'But I thought you said we weren't to leave her at home alone with Carl.'

My mother slapped him across the back of his head and hissed angrily, 'I told you not to talk about it in front of her.' Then she turned to look over her shoulder at me.

I stared into her eyes for a moment, and then said, 'It's all right. I'm going to stay out here. I won't go in the house.' And as I sat and watched them walk up the road, I wondered what my mother could have meant.

She'd caught Carl on at least a couple of occasions with his hands down my trousers when he was playing one of his 'games'. Her tone had been sharp when she'd asked him what he was doing. But he'd pretended he hadn't noticed the look she was giving him and he'd answered jovially, 'Just playing,' or 'Just keeping our hands warm.' She'd looked at me then, before turning away and walking out of the room, presumably deciding to ignore a possibility she didn't want to have to face.

A couple of years later, I heard her tell a houseful of drunks that if anyone ever raped or attacked me, she wouldn't report it to the police, because she wouldn't want me to have to go through the trauma of standing up in court to give evidence. At the time, I thought it was an odd thing for her to say, but I wonder now if it was her way of trying to convince herself she'd done the right thing when she decided not to rock the already unstable boat that was our household by asking questions when she'd rather not hear the answers.

Living with Carl taught me not to trust anyone. Gradually, I built a wall around myself in an attempt to prevent anyone being able to hurt me. However, it was a wall that also prevented anyone getting close to me. The hugs and kisses I'd always had from my grandparents had been very important to me, not least because they'd seemed like affirmation of the fact that I was loved, and therefore lovable. But by the time I was eight or nine years old I refused to let even my grandparents touch me. If I was left alone in a room with one of the uncles who'd been so good to me from the day I was born, I'd get up and walk out, just in case they came too close. When I'd lived with my grandparents, I'd been almost constantly cheerful and affectionate, but now I came across as a cold, heartless little girl who loved no one and who never showed her feelings, whether happy or sad. Everyone must have thought I hated them. But it was all a front, a carefully erected barrier to hide behind so that no one else could hurt me.

I had no one to talk to or confide in. My mother was always drunk, high on pills, or both, and in any case she didn't care what I thought or how I felt. She had no energy or interest to spare for anyone but herself. One of the things I particularly hated was rushing home from school bursting to tell her about something that had happened during the day, and finding she was already drunk. My heart would sink, because I knew there was absolutely no point trying to talk to her. And even if I did manage to make her listen to me, she'd misunderstand whatever it was I was saying and it wouldn't be long before she flew into a rage and attacked me.

My mother had obviously told Carl about her life before she met him – at least, *her* version of its events. In fact, she related to anyone who'd listen the exaggerated details of all the hardships she'd had to bear. Whereas, in reality, most of her problems were self-inflicted, the result of too much alcohol and not taking her medication properly. I think the main reason she talked about them was because she loved the attention she received when she told people how my father used to beat her up and how he had never loved me, his first child and his only daughter. She didn't care at all for my sake about my father not liking me; she just enjoyed basking in reflected sympathy when she ladled on the pathos and described how miserable it was for her poor little girl, and how brutal and aggressive my father had been towards *her* because of his hatred of me.

I would feel physically sick when she talked about it. Not just because I hated her discussing me with total strangers and because it made me feel as though there was something wrong with me if my own father couldn't love me, but also because I knew that Carl valued any knowledge he could glean about me that would give him ammunition when he taunted me. He often accused me of ruining my mother's life, and would thrust a nicotine-stained finger into my face as he blamed me for her alcoholism and for all her mental health problems – while choosing to overlook the fact that if she hadn't been a mentally ill alcoholic, she'd certainly never have got herself tied up with a grizzled, ugly no-hoper like him.

I was nine years old when my mother's behaviour changed from erratic to dangerous, and she was sectioned for four months. She was in hospital over Easter, and I used the little bit of money I'd saved up to buy her a box of three creme eggs. I gave them to her when we went to see her at the hospital, and she was really pleased. She opened the box immediately and insisted on giving one to me, one to my brother and keeping one for herself. It was the sort of thing a normal mother might do, and it was one of the moments when I realised I loved her, despite everything.

Although I had precious little evidence to support the idea that she loved Chris and me, I think she did, as much as she was able to feel affection for anyone. Like everything else about her, though, her love was erratic. When she was sober, she could sometimes be like a proper mother – which always drove Carl crazy. He hated it when she was nice to us, because caring about *us* meant diverting her attention away from *him*, and he'd behave like a spoilt, jealous little boy.

That day in the hospital, when she was nice to Chris and me, I think she was missing us, possibly for the first time in her life. I was certainly missing *her*; I *really* wanted her to come home, and to be like that all the time. So I felt particularly miserable when we left her there and walked back through the sterile, empty hospital corridors towards the exit.

As soon as we got into the car, I burst into tears and Carl turned on me immediately, shouting, 'Shut your fucking mouth. I don't know why you're crying in any case; you're the reason your mother's locked up in a mental hospital.'

All the way home, he continued to taunt me, saying, 'Your mother only drinks because of you,' and 'Even your own father hates you.' Then he turned to my brother, who was sitting in the passenger seat beside him, and said, 'If it wasn't for your sister, your mum wouldn't be ill and she wouldn't be in that godforsaken dump of a hospital. She'd be safe at home with us.'

At first my brother just looked unhappy, but, with Carl's persistent encouragement, he soon began to torment me too, and to tease me because I was crying.

It was just one more step towards my already almost complete acceptance of the fact that I was responsible for everything bad in my mother's life – which meant just about every aspect of it. If I hadn't been born, she wouldn't be a hopeless, abandoned alcoholic and she wouldn't have the mental health problems, which, amongst other things, prevented her from ever being happy or contented. I was guilty, and it was no wonder my father hated me too.

However, although Carl apparently despised me for ruining my mother's life, he still abused me sexually and, while she was in hospital, he seemed to take great pleasure in doing it in the bed he normally shared with her. He'd come into my room every night, lift me out of my bed and carry me into their bedroom. If I woke up, I'd soon fall fast asleep again when he put me down on his bed. But he'd take hold of my hand and place my fingers around his penis. He tried to teach me what he wanted me to do, but every time he took his hand away from mine, I let go, and he'd curse at me and start all over again. Eventually, it became easier just to do what he wanted and try to get it over with as quickly as possible. Also, although I didn't know what he was doing at the time, he often tried to have full inter-course with me. But I'd scream out in pain and push him away.

Every night he kept me awake for hours, abusing me again and again until I was so exhausted I'd fall fast asleep on top of him. I'd try to slide my body off him so that I could lie with my head on the pillow, but he'd keep dragging me back into position until he'd finished. Sometimes, I'd wake up to find myself lying beside him, naked and without any memory of how I got there, and my stomach would churn as I wondered what he'd done to me while I slept.

Every morning, Carl's alarm went off in time for him to send me back to my bedroom before Chris woke up, so that we could get dressed and set off to school together, like normal children. On a couple of mornings, though, Chris woke up first and saw me coming out of Carl's bedroom. The first time it happened his expression was a mixture of disbelief and disgust as he asked, 'Did you sleep in there – with Carl?' I felt my face burning with embarrassment as I denied it. And then Carl came out of the bedroom behind me and said, 'She had a nightmare, so she came into my room' – as though that would have been the most normal thing in the world for me to have done.

Afterwards, on the way to school, my brother laughed at me and teased me for getting into bed with 'that disgusting old man'. I shrugged off his accusation, pretending I didn't care. But the truth was that it upset me, because I felt he should have known I hated Carl so much I'd rather have been ripped apart and eaten by the monster we used to imagine lurked in the corner of the bedroom we used to share than have willingly spent a single night in Carl's bed.

Despite his occasional teasing, my brother was the only person I really loved and trusted, and we were very close. There was no point trying to tell him about what Carl was doing to me, because he was too young to understand. But on any other topic he was the one person I could talk to, because he was sharing most of my experiences. Although we couldn't protect each other physically, we *were* able to give each other emotional support and, with Chris there, at least I wasn't alone.

However, Chris was as troubled as I was, and his bed-wetting was just one of many manifestations of his deep distress and unhappiness. He'd been kicked out of nursery school because his behaviour was already uncontrollable, and he became more destructive and aggressive as he got older.

'You're vicious, just like your fucking father,' my mother used to scream at him, and she eventually tried to have him put into care. I assume it was on the grounds that he was beyond her control, although I can't imagine the reasons why social services decided he was better off staying with her. She was always telling him that as soon as he was old enough, she was going to make him join the army; then she'd wind herself up into a tightly coiled spring of fury and frustration when nothing she said seemed to have any effect on him. But I could see beneath his tough exterior, and I think I was the only person who understood how profoundly hurt and miserable he really was.

Remarkably, although my mother tried to get Chris taken into care, for some reason no one ever reported *her* to the social services, not even her doctor, who must have known exactly what she was like. Years later, a family that lived in our street had very similar problems to the ones we had when Chris and I were young, and some of the neighbours got together to discuss whether they should report the mother to social services. But they decided eventually to do nothing, on the basis that 'some kids are happy living in their own shit'. So I suppose that's what people thought about us – that we were simply 'a bad lot' who were best avoided and left to our own devices. And although ours was clearly a very dysfunctional and unhappy family, no one ever really knew what was going on *inside* our house, particularly because Chris and I would always lie and back up my mother's repeated and indignantly determined claim that she never drank and that everything at home was fine.

But although we never discussed our lives at home with anyone else, Chris and I did talk to each other, and I don't think I'd have been able to cope at all throughout the months when my mother was in hospital if I hadn't had his support.

9

Trying – and failing

WHEN MY MOTHER came out of hospital on that occasion, she was a completely different person. When she was drunk, she was only interested in Carl and in where her next drink was coming from. But she'd stopped drinking, which seemed to have allowed the bit of her that cared about my brother and me to dry out, and she wanted to spend time with us. Although I was nervous to begin with, waiting for her to revert to what, for her, was normal behaviour and start shouting and lashing out at me, it didn't happen, and I gradually began to allow myself to believe that she might really have changed.

Of course, Carl had a very different view of things, although he was far too sly and manipulative to come right out and say so. Instead, he'd come home from work every evening with a bottle of Bacardi, open it in front of my mother and inhale dramatically, as though he could smell something wonderful. Then he'd pour some into one of the crystal glasses, take a sip and sigh with exaggerated pleasure, before almost pleading with my mother, 'Go on, Judith, have a drink. Just one won't hurt. You deserve it after everything you've had to put up with. Go on. Just one.'

He hated her being sober, and he hated the fact that it upset his carefully organised routine: if she wasn't drunk, he couldn't continue to sneak into my bedroom every night without getting caught. So he'd go on and on at her, and I'd sit with my fingers crossed, thinking, 'Please don't drink it, Mum; please don't drink it,' although I didn't have the guts to say it out loud in front of him.

Chris and I did plead with her as soon as Carl was out of the room, though, and she promised us faithfully that she wouldn't drink again. But it didn't take long for her to give in. I suppose it was amazing she held out for as long as she did. She'd been dependent on alcohol since her early teens – and she'd probably drunk it every single day since then, except when she'd been in hospital – and the truth was that there was little else in her life by that time.

As I watched her take the first drink, it felt as though a dead weight had settled in the pit of my stomach. For a few precious days, she'd talked and listened to me. I'd even told her about something that had happened at school and she'd laughed, and for a moment she'd been part of my life in the way I'd always longed for her to be. But as soon as she lifted the glass to her lips, it was all over.

Carl must have known how I'd be feeling, because he smirked at me behind my mother's back as if he'd won some stupid, childish contest against me, when in fact what he'd actually done was condemn my mother to living the life of a hopeless drunk. Whichever way you looked at it, it wasn't much of a victory, but particularly when your opponent was a nine-year-old child who just wanted her mother to care about her, even if it was only a little bit.

The next day, when my mother had sobered up, she was upset about giving in so easily, and she begged Chris and me not to let her drink again.

'You *have* to help me,' she pleaded. 'Whatever happens, whatever I say, *don't* let me have a drink. I won't let you down again, I promise.'

She probably meant it when she said it, but ever since she was a little girl herself, I don't think anyone had ever managed to prevent her doing anything she'd made up her mind to do. And the next time she drank and I reminded her about what she'd said, she shouted at me and told me to 'mind your own fucking business'. I sat in my bedroom and sobbed. I didn't understand how she could care so little about my brother and me that she'd choose drink instead of us. On the days she'd been sober, she'd almost been like a *real* mother and I'd loved her. But it seemed she hadn't felt the same way, and she didn't really love us at all.

However, Carl was delighted that everything had returned to 'normal'. He wanted my mother to be in a more or less permanently drunken state, even though he blamed me whenever she stopped taking her medication and either rose into the stratosphere on a cloud of mania, or sank into the depths of a deep depression. 'You're a fucking useless little bastard. It's *your* fault she's ill,' he'd shout at me. And although I'd long ago accepted the fact that virtually everything bad *was* my fault, I couldn't really understand how it could be the case this time, when *he* was the one to have almost forced drink down her throat.

My mother hated taking the pills that helped control her mood swings. I don't know whether she stopped taking them because they made her bloated and caused her to put on weight, which they did, or whether it was because after she'd been taking them for a while she began to feel better and thought she didn't need them any more. Whatever the reason, it meant that, from an early age, I had to take responsibility for her medication. I'd go to the doctor's surgery to collect her tablets and then count them out for her and try to make sure she took them when she was supposed to. She was devious about it though – as she was about everything – and she was clever at convincing me she'd taken them when she hadn't. So her mood swings combined with her drinking made her almost impossible to live with.

By the age of nine, I'd become the adult in our house in many ways. While my friends were playing, I'd be cleaning and tidying with a single-mindedness that bordered on the obsessive – scrubbing and bleaching the floors and cupboards, cleaning up after Carl and my mother, and washing, ironing and cooking for my brother and me. It was my coping mechanism – the only aspect of my chaotic, horrible life that I could exert any control over – and I was also convinced that if our house was clean, we could fool people into thinking we were normal, just like them.

My mother, on the other hand, rarely cleaned anything, however filthy it was, except when she was having one of her manic episodes. When she was manic, she'd often stay up for days on end, and sometimes the first indication that something was wrong would be when she started vacuuming the house in the early hours of the morning. Then she'd scrub the floors, empty out cupboards and drawers and try to wash the horrible, disgusting black mould off the window frames.

She'd been having a manic episode for a couple of days when I woke up one morning, pushed back my bedcovers and knelt on my bed so that I could reach across and lift a corner of the curtain. What I saw when I looked out of the window nearly made me fall off the end of the bed in amazement. The back garden had been completely transformed. When I'd gone to sleep the previous night, it had contained its usual array of dead and dying plants, which made it look like the backdrop to a film about the aftermath of some devastating chemical attack. But this morning the borders were stuffed full of shrubs with brightly coloured flowers and fat, healthy-looking leaves. They covered almost every inch of the soil, so that the backyard looked just like a proper garden – in fact, like the garden at my grandparents' house, instead of a depressing patch of wasteland.

Then, as I gazed out at it, my stomach began to churn. What could have happened to create this oasis in the desert? In my experience, change was rarely something that occurred for 'good' reasons. And, as it turned out, I was right. Fuelled by a bout of mania in the middle of the night, my mother had crept into all our neighbours' gardens and helped herself to any plants that caught her fancy, bringing them home, one by one, and transplanting them into our shrivelled, weed-infested wilderness.

It ended – as my mother's ideas so often did – with lots of angry shouting, and it wasn't long before our briefly magnificent garden was returned to its more usual state of barren gloom.

The longer my mother's manic episodes lasted, the more abnormal and psychotic her behaviour became. And, inevitably, Chris and I suffered the consequences, which included the backlash from people who didn't dare confront her directly. She was always threatening to sort people out, and she'd often expand the threat by telling them, 'You better not upset me, because my daughter's mad and she'll come after you when you're not looking and stab you in the back with a knife.' So it was largely thanks to her that I gained the bad reputation that caused me to have so much trouble with people on the estate.

Another thing she did fairly regularly was telephone the school, shouting and swearing at the teachers and telling them she was 'coming down there to sort you out'. Then someone would come into my classroom, glance at me briefly while whispering something to my teacher and I'd be called out and told to go to the head teacher's office. Then I'd wait in the corridor, kicking my feet nervously and trying to look as though I didn't care, while I wondered what could have happened this time.

Eventually, the head teacher would open the door of her office and tell me, in a tightly irritated voice, to go in. She'd ask me to explain my mother's latest abusive phone call, questioning me about what I might have told her that would have upset her so much and caused her to telephone the school, cursing and screaming. It was a question for which there was never any answer: why did my mother do any of the inexplicably strange and embarrassing things she did? But, inevitably – and unfairly – it seemed that I was considered to be as much to blame as she was for her threatening, aggressive behaviour.

When I lived with my grandparents, I knew without really thinking about it what 'normal behaviour' was. Without their influence, though, I gradually just accepted that the life I led with my mother and Carl must lie somewhere else on the spectrum of normality. And then, sometimes, something would happen to make me realise that certain aspects of it, at least, weren't really normal at all.

For example, one Saturday afternoon, after I'd stayed overnight at a friend's house and was getting ready to go home, her mother asked me, 'Is someone coming to pick you up, Anna?'

'No…' I answered cautiously, not really sure what she meant.

'In that case, we'll walk home with you,' she said.

'Oh, that's okay,' I told her. I felt uncomfortable and slightly suspicious of her motives, as I so often did if anyone ever offered to do something nice for me – which happened increasingly rarely as I got older.

'No, no. We'll come with you,' she insisted. 'You're

much too young to be walking around on your own, particularly in the streets round here.'

No one ever walked anywhere with me at any time of the day or night, and it had never crossed my mind that it might be something other parents did.

When we got to my house, my mother answered the door and stood staring at me, as if trying to remember who I was. It was about three o'clock in the afternoon, but it was clear she was already drunk, although she managed to focus on my friend's mother for a moment, before muttering something incoherent and going back into the living room and shutting the door.

Embarrassed, I glanced quickly at my friend's mother. She had a grim look on her face, although she smiled a tight smile as she turned towards me and said, 'Run upstairs and get some clean clothes. I'm taking you home to stay the night with us.'

'I thought she wasn't allowed to stay another night,' my friend said, before adding hastily, 'Not that I'm complaining!'

I was already running up the stairs, afraid her mother might change her mind, but I heard her whisper, 'Well, I'm certainly not leaving the poor child in *this* house for the weekend.'

I HATED CARL for encouraging my mother to start

drinking again after she came out of hospital. Without him, she might at least have had a chance to stop and get well. I wanted her to be well for her own sake, so that she didn't die. But I also longed for her to be a 'proper' mother and, perhaps most importantly of all, to be sober enough to realise what Carl was doing to me and to protect me against his abuse.

Gradually, I became obsessed with the belief that *everything* was Carl's fault and, after discussing it with my brother, I decided we should try to kill him.

The first plan I came up with was to stuff mud and stones into the exhaust pipe of his car, which I thought would result in the car blowing up while he was driving to work. I don't know where the idea came from – perhaps it was something I'd seen on television – but somehow he discovered what I'd done and I got belted for putting his life in danger. On the plus side, though, his reaction did seem to confirm that it *was* something that might kill him, so I repeated the process again a few weeks later – unfortunately, with the same result.

On another occasion, I decided to try to blind him by folding up little pink gun caps and hiding them underneath the remnants of tobacco in the bowl of his pipe. The next time he picked up his pipe, he added some more tobacco to what was already in there – as he always did – and then he lit a match and set fire to it. As the heat slowly spread through the tobacco, the caps began to explode in his face. Disappointingly, I wasn't there to witness it, although I know he was shocked. Apparently, he shouted at my mother, but as I wasn't punished for it, it was clear that he never worked out what had happened. I was delighted at the thought that I'd made him afraid, even if it had only been for a few minutes.

After a while, though, it became clear that attempting to get rid of Carl by killing him wasn't going to work. So I decided to approach the problem from another angle and try to put my mother off him. The first idea I came up with was to make her see just what a repulsive old man he really was.

One evening, while they were drinking and watching television together in the living room, I went into the kitchen and made a mixture of vinegar and pepper in a glass. Then I crept up the stairs and into their bedroom, where I poured it over the crotch of Carl's pyjamas and all over his side of the bed. I watched with a sense of spiteful pleasure as the yellow stain spread across the sheet and formed a mark that looked exactly like I'd hoped it would. I was certain that when my mother saw it she'd think he'd wet himself and she'd be so disgusted she wouldn't want anything more to do with him.

In the event, though, that plan didn't work any better than my attempts to kill or maim him, and it was beginning to look as though there was nothing I was going to be able to do to get rid of him.

Between them, Carl and my mother had snatched away my childhood and given me in return a sense of hopelessness that never left me, and a warped, confused understanding of what love is that was to ruin my life for years and that still remains with me to this day.

Love was a word that was rarely mentioned in our house, except by Carl after he'd sexually abused me and was insisting I should tell him I loved him. It was clear to me that I was unlovable. My father hated me and my mother was, at best, indifferent to me, because she only really cared about alcohol. She'd look at me sometimes with pure hatred in her eyes and scream, 'You're nothing but a cold, hard bitch. Why don't you just fuck off?' When she was sober, she never, ever, told me she loved me. And, when I thought about it, it was obvious she didn't, because otherwise she wouldn't have made so many attempts to kill herself, which, if she succeeded, would mean leaving my brother and me all alone. Paradoxically, though, when she was drunk and depressed, she'd sometimes stroke my hair and sob and tell me over and over again how much she loved me.

Consequently, I was confused about what loving some-one really meant, and I learned to accept that the love I used to think existed wasn't real. What love actually seemed to involve was letting someone have sex with you when you didn't want them to, even when what they did to you left you feeling miserably defeated and bullied.

No matter how hard I tried to please her, my mother persisted in telling everyone and anyone who'd listen that I was a nasty piece of work. Carl took every opportunity to encourage her dislike of me and would often tell her what a vindictive little bitch I was – largely, I realise now, in order to cover himself in case I ever told her what he'd been doing to me. And I think it was at least part of the reason why my mother grew closer to my brother than to me.

Sometimes, she gave me a really good hiding, but usually only when she thought I'd been nasty to Chris. I can remember several occasions when she chased me as I ran up the stairs with my heart pounding and managed to lock myself in the bathroom. She'd be thumping on the door with her fists, screaming and swearing at me, and then suddenly she'd stop. For a few minutes, she'd stay completely quiet, and then her voice would be kind and coaxing as she said, 'It's all right. I know you didn't mean to be nasty to him. You can come out now. I'm not cross any more. I promise I won't hurt you.'

After a while, I'd open the bathroom door cautiously and poke my head out, and she'd grab me by the hair, drag me on to the landing and beat me viciously. Then she'd leave me leaning against the wall and sobbing, as she stomped back down the stairs.

One day, when I was playing with the little girl next door, Chris was annoying us by insisting on following us all round the estate. Eventually, I went into the kitchen with my friend and complained to my mother: 'Mu-um, can you stop Chris following us? We want to play on our own.'

Without warning, she raised her hand and slapped me as hard as she could across the face. The room started spinning and my head was knocked sideways so sharply I thought my neck was going to snap. I was still reeling from the shock when my mother turned on my friend and screamed at her, 'Fuck off out of my house and don't fucking come back.' The girl burst into tears and was still sobbing loudly and struggling to open the back door when my mother shouted at me, 'You're a nasty fucking bitch. Fuck off upstairs to bed.'

I felt faint, and sick with humiliation, and I thought my head was going to burst as I ran up the stairs and threw myself down on my bed. All I'd asked her to do was stop my little brother following us around – and the irony was that I loved him far more than she could ever love anyone. I sat on my bed, crying and thinking angrily that if I *was* the cold, hard bitch my mother was always telling me I was, she and Carl were the ones who had made me that way.

I still didn't understand what Carl was doing to me when he came to my bedroom almost every night. But if my mother had bothered to sober up long enough to spend a bit of time with me, she might have realised that her boyfriend was sexually abusing me, and that I had good reason to hate everyone. I despised my father, I loathed Carl with a passion, and I only really loved my mother against my will and better judgement, because she let me down time and time again. I loved my grandparents, but it felt as though they'd abandoned me, which was a feeling my mother was always careful to encourage.

I was convinced I was worthless. And I was very lonely. But I was completely unable to change the situation I was in, and my hatred did me no good, because, in reality, I was the only one to suffer as it nibbled away at my soul.

Every night, I lay in my bed after Carl had left my room and prayed to God to let me die in my sleep. If I'd been offered three wishes at that time, I'd have said, three times, 'Don't let me wake up in the morning.'

We lived our lives on a battlefield of constant conflict and chaos, and I rarely asked anyone to come home with me. Although my closest friends were all from dysfunctional families, ours was by far the worst, and if anyone did come round after school, my mother and Carl would invariably be drunk. And, as if that wasn't embarrassment enough for me, my mother would announce to my bewildered friend that she had just come out of 'the nut house' and was quite mad. If the friend was a girl, Carl would stare at her breasts and say things like, 'They look nice,' and to boys he'd give a knowing wink and ask, 'Did you know that the left hand is the dirty hand?' They'd have absolutely no idea what he was talking about. So they'd smile small, nervous smiles and shuffle their feet awkwardly, and I'd feel their discomfort rising off them like heat.

I spent all the long, lonely, unhappy hours of my life either at school, at home, or sitting with my brother outside one pub after another. More or less the only other thing we ever did was go to the local swimming pool, which I dreaded just as much as I dreaded everything else. Because taking us to the pool was simply another excuse for Carl to exercise his perversions and leer at all the young girls in their swimming costumes. Chris and I provided him with the ideal 'cover': who would suspect a cheerful man who's swimming and laughing with his own two children of being a pervert?

He'd pretend to be teaching me how to swim, when in fact he'd have one hand underneath me, on my stomach, and the other between my legs. As he forced his fingers inside my swimming costume and touched me, he'd call out jovial comments and sweep me through the water with a false, fixed smile on his face. He knew I'd be too embarrassed to make a scene in public, and he seemed to get an added thrill from doing what he did just inches away from where my mother and brother were jumping up and down in the water.

For me, being abused in a public place in front of dozens of people was the final humiliation, and confirmation of the fact that I was completely powerless in every way. As Carl joked and smiled, I'd know that I was trapped until he decided to release me. I'd be almost rigid with terror at the thought that someone might see what he was doing, and I can still remember the look of horror on the face of the young boy who one day did realise that Carl's hand was between my legs and *inside* my swimming costume.

Carl never seemed to tire of thinking up new ways to abuse and control me, and one night, when he and my mother ran out of Bacardi, he insisted on driving to the off-licence to buy some more. As time passed, it seemed to take more alcohol to render my mother unconscious, but she must already have been too drunk – or too indifferent – to argue when he told her he was going to take me with him.

My pleas to be left at home were simply wasted breath, and as soon as we reached the dark, winding back roads away from the estate, he told me to sit on his knee. I was wary, as I always was of anything Carl told me to do, but he reassured me, 'Come on. There are no other cars around. I thought you'd like to steer.'

I was going to learn to drive a car! I could hardly believe Carl was offering to do something so exciting, and I clambered around the gearstick and slipped on to his knee behind the steering wheel. He showed me how to position my hands and how to turn the wheel just a little bit so that we didn't swerve all over the road. And then he put his own hands up my skirt and into my knickers and I could feel his penis pressing up against me.

I began to squirm, trying to get him off me. But he pressed his foot a little harder on the accelerator and shouted, 'Look out! Don't let go of the steering wheel! We're going to crash!' And instinctively I stopped struggling and tightened my grip on the wheel.

On the way home, he told me to sit on his lap again, but I refused.

'Come on,' he wheedled. 'I'll let you drive. I won't do anything this time. I won't touch you. I promise.'

So I climbed back on to his knee and he put his hand back inside my knickers.

When you're a child, you *want* to trust people; and, if you don't, you're easily made to feel that the fault lies with you. So when an adult says 'Trust me', you believe again and again that this time you can; this time they're telling the truth and they won't trick or hurt you. And each time they do the thing that past experience should have told you they would do, you feel a little bit more stupid and you come one step nearer to believing nothing good ever really happens in life and no one can be trusted.

After that first time, Carl did the same thing every time he made me go in the car with him to the off-licence. The only difference was that he didn't bother cajoling me into going or lying about his reasons for letting me steer the car. He simply ordered me out of the house and smirked at me as I climbed reluctantly on to the passenger seat beside him.

My mother was sectioned again a few months after the last time, and again she came out of hospital swearing she'd given up alcohol for good. This time, though, she held out against Carl's attempts to break her resolve. But because she was of little use to him when she was sober – and perhaps because *she* saw *him* in a different light when her faculties weren't clouded by drink – their relationship became increasingly strained, until eventually she threw him out.

And that was the beginning of a new and previously unimaginable era in our lives. My mother still had mood swings, although they weren't nearly as bad or as violent as they had been when she was drunk – she hadn't suddenly become a saint by any means – and I could sometimes talk to her. Most importantly of all, however, with Carl no longer there, I could sleep unmolested and unafraid in my bed at night. It was like starting a new life.

And then, when I was eleven years old, my grandfather died from the cancer he'd been fighting for the last few years. I was devastated. He'd always been one of the few solid things in my life. Even when I didn't see him very often, I could conjure up the kind expression in his eyes and the deep, reassuring tone of his voice whenever I needed comfort. For the last couple of years I hadn't been as nice to him as I used to be, not because I loved him any less than I'd always done, but because I'd learned to be afraid of talking to anyone in case I spilled one of my mother's – or Carl's – secrets, and I'd withdrawn further and further behind a cool, indifferent facade. Now he'd gone, and I'd never sit on his knee again, or have the chance to tell him that I'd never stopped loving him.

His death left a vacuum in all our lives – a vacuum that Carl decided to use to his advantage. When he heard that my grandfather had died, he got in touch with my mother and somehow managed to persuade her to let him come back and stay with us – 'Just for a while, so that I can help you to get over the shock of your father's death and get back on your feet.'

He'd been in the house less than ten minutes when he said, 'Come on, Judith, have a little drink. You look so miserable. It'll make you feel better. You deserve a drink after all you've been through. Just one won't hurt you.'

I wanted to throw myself on top of him and scratch his eyes out with my bare hands. My brother and I needed our mother to be strong for us, not crying and rambling incoherently and trying to drink herself into an early grave. But there was nothing I could do. By the end of the night she lay drunk and oblivious on the sofa in the living room, and things had returned to normal.

It was shortly after that, when I was in my last year of primary school, that I saw a programme on television about rape. It came on while I was sitting in the living room with Carl and my mother, and I squirmed with embarrassment as we watched it. But it wasn't until a few days later, when I was in a class at school, half-listening to the monotonous drone of my teacher's voice, that it hit me like a physical blow: *that* was what Carl had been doing to me!

I thought I was going to be sick. For all those years since the night when my mother had dragged Chris and me from our grandparents' house, Carl had been having sex with me. All the horrible, painful things he'd been doing were all part of sex. I couldn't believe it. And I couldn't understand it. Why? Why would he do that to me, a child, particularly as he'd presumably also been doing the same thing to my mother?

A sour-tasting liquid burned my throat as it rose into my mouth, and I felt my cheeks flush with shame. No one must find out. If my grandmother, aunts and uncles were to know, they'd hate me. It was difficult enough knowing that they thought my behaviour was odd and unfriendly, but it would be more than I could bear if they were to despise and be disgusted by me. That was something I didn't think I could live with.

I made a decision then and there never to tell anyone about what Carl had been doing. I'd kept my feelings locked up inside me for five years, until I found it virtually impossible to express myself in any coherent way. So I was used to having a secret inner life, and this was just one more horrible thing to keep to myself. I wouldn't think about it or try to deal with it; I'd bury it deep inside me, build a wall around it and ignore it, and in time it would simply disappear.

A COUPLE OF days later, I was in my mother's bedroom, putting some washing in the laundry basket, when Carl sneaked up behind me, put his arms around my waist and tried to pull me down on to the bed.

'Get off me! Let go!' I hissed at him, a warm sense of satisfaction spreading through my body as I saw the look of surprised disbelief on his face. 'Let go of me,' I said again, this time speaking the words slowly and clearly, as if to a child. 'Or I will tell my mum.'

'What are you going to tell her?' he asked, recovering

from his initial shock and sneering at me. 'Go on, tell me what you're going to say to her.'

I hadn't had time to think that through, but I managed to sound more sure of myself than I felt as I said, 'I haven't decided yet.' Then I walked out of the room, leaving Carl staring after me in dismay. And that was the last time he ever tried to touch me.

There was little to keep him with us after that. It was time for him to move on. But he wasn't going to go without one last act of spite.

A few days later, when he was in my mother's bedroom, packing his clothes into a battered old suitcase, he called down the stairs to me. I was sitting on the sofa watching television with Chris, and I looked at him and shrugged before walking out of the room and up the stairs.

I stood in the doorway to the bedroom and could see that there were photographs strewn all over the bed. Carl picked some of them up and held them out towards me.

'Look,' he said, grinning and pushing them into my hands as I stepped forward. 'It's your mum. I'm taking them with me, but I thought you'd like to see them before I go.'

I looked down at the photographs and gasped, dropping them back on to the bed as if they'd burned my fingers. Carl stood up, grabbed my head with one hand and held one of the pictures in front of my eyes, forcing me to look at the disgusting, explicit image of him and my mother.

'Look at them! Look!' he shouted, hooking his fingers into my hair and pushing my head down towards the bed and all the other repulsive images that will remain with me for ever. Then he scooped them all up, dumped them into his suitcase and stomped down the stairs and out of the front door.

10

As one door opens, another one shuts

AFTER HE LEFT, Carl kept phoning my mother and begging her to let him come back. It seemed, though, that when she was sober she could see what everyone else could see – that he was an unattractive, much older man who had very little to offer her – and she stayed firm in her resolve to live without him and to try to turn her life around.

One evening, I was in the living room with my mother when the phone rang. She was lying on the sofa watching TV, and she reached out with one hand and picked up the receiver. I could tell immediately it was Carl again. I could hear the tinny quack of his voice and I assumed he was doing his usual embarrassing pleading. My mother didn't say anything for a while, but then she interrupted him by saying, 'I've been talking to Tracy.' For a few seconds, they were both silent and then she added, in a completely different, angry, tone of voice, 'She tells me you went round there one night when I was away and told her something about taking Anna's virginity.'

A cold, prickly sweat broke out over my entire body and I felt sick. Wiping the dampness from my hands on to my skirt, I got to my feet and left the room without a word. My mother hadn't even looked at me while she was speaking, but I felt humiliated and confused. Although she'd sounded angry with Carl, she'd also seemed jealous, as though she resented me in the same way she might resent an adult woman who Carl wanted to have sex with.

What also bemused me was that, despite the fact Tracy was a single mother with a little girl of her own, she'd had that conversation with Carl and then decided to keep it to herself until after my mother had thrown him out of the house. Hadn't she wondered at all about what he might be doing to me, and thought that perhaps it was something she should mention to my mother immediately? In fairness, though, I expect she was probably as frightened as everyone else of my mother's rages – so frightened, it seems, that she'd chosen to abandon me to a sick pervert like Carl rather than risk being the subject of one of her tirades.

I sat on my bed with my fists tightly clenched as I waited for my mother to come upstairs and ask me if Carl had ever tried to touch me. It seemed that the moment I'd been half-wanting, half-dreading for so long had finally arrived: I was going to tell someone what Carl had been doing to me. It was far too late now for talking about it to do any good, because he'd already left. But at least someone would know, and perhaps sharing the terrible secret I'd been holding inside me for so long would make it lose its power over me, and stop the flow of poison that was spreading into every corner of my life.

I tried to decide how I felt about what was going to happen. Was I more afraid than relieved? Was there a part of me that was delighted by the thought of how angry my mother was going to be with Carl? But my mother never came, and she never again mentioned what she'd said on the phone to Carl. Clearly, what he'd been doing to me didn't matter, because *I* didn't matter, not even to my own mother.

Carl hadn't been gone long before she'd started drinking heavily again, and when a bar opened in a new community centre on the estate – just a short drunken stagger away from our house – she couldn't believe her luck. She began to go there every night, arriving when the bar opened and leaving when it shut, and she made a whole group of new friends amongst the other alcoholics and misfits who did the same. At weekends, she'd go at lunchtime and stay until it closed at three o'clock in the afternoon; then she'd come home, fall into a drunken sleep on the sofa and wake up just in time to go out again when it re-opened at seven in the evening.

While she was asleep, Chris and I would creep silently around the house, hoping that if we didn't wake her, she might sleep right through and not go out again in the evening. But although she appeared to be completely dead to the world, she had some sort of internal alarm clock that woke her up just before seven every night, however drunk she'd been when she came in.

When she wasn't causing trouble at my school or amongst our neighbours, lying unconscious in our living room, or drinking herself into a state of oblivion at the bar, my mother would often disappear with someone who told her they had drink back at their place. Sometimes, she'd turn up miles away from home at a party where she knew no one and had no means of getting back again. When she did finally come home, drunk and with no memory of where she'd been, she'd take a handful of sleeping tablets and sink into a coma that could last for days. And, in some ways, those were the 'best' times, because those were the times when I knew where she was and I could take care of her. As soon as she'd passed out, my brother and I would gently lift up her head and place a pillow underneath it before covering her with a blanket. Sometimes, she'd be on the sofa and sometimes on the floor, and we'd leave her where she was, stepping over her or creeping silently around her for the next couple of days, terrified of disturbing her and praying she wouldn't wake up and disappear again before she was sober.

Despite the misery she caused in my life, I loved my mother, and at least when she was at home and unconscious, I knew she was safe. Whereas when she was out drinking, she could be anywhere, lying hurt or even dead, and she might never come home again. Trying to keep her alive became the focus of my existence, and the responsibility of it helped to destroy the small part of my childhood that she and Carl hadn't already ruined.

My mother developed an 'impressive' reputation amongst her drunken friends because of the amount of alcohol she could consume before she passed out. She'd eat as little as possible, drink a substantial amount and then make herself sick so that she had room in her stomach for more of the pints and pints of lager she swallowed until she literally couldn't fit any more in. Then she'd disappear into the toilet, make herself sick again, and return, with her face red and blotchy, to start the process all over from the beginning. Once she tired of drinking lager, she'd move on to doubles, and then, eventually, she'd pass out and either be brought home by someone who knew her or taken to hospital by an ambulance called by the bar staff.

It wasn't long before her drinking was so completely out of control that she lost her job – for arriving back from lunch drunk once too often. She'd wake up every morning confused and disorientated, with her whole body shaking so violently from the DTs that she couldn't even lift a cup to her mouth without spilling its contents. Then she'd have some 'hair of the dog', which would calm her down enough for her to get ready to go back to the bar as soon as it opened at lunchtime.

I can remember going to the town with a friend during one lunch hour when I was at school and bumping into my mother and *her* friend, who were on their way to the pub. Years of drinking had caused my mother's body to become bloated and she looked a mess. We stopped to speak to them, but I was uncomfortable and anxious not to hang around long enough for my mother to say something embarrassing. Then, as we were turning to go our separate ways, my friend – who lived in a nice house with nice, respectable parents – asked, 'Is that your mum?' My mother and her friend were still within earshot when, like the apostle Peter, I answered, 'No. No, it isn't.' I could hear the hurt in my mother's voice as she called my name, and my friend was clearly bemused when she realised I'd lied.

What was even worse than the fact that my mother was out every evening, leaving Chris and me alone at home for hours on end, was the constant stream of drunken strangers she began to bring back with her from the bar to continue drinking and taking drugs at our house. She'd always preferred to drink in the company of other people, regardless of who they were, and it made no difference to her that Chris and I had to get up and go to school the next morning. Night after night we'd be woken up by the sound of people shouting and laughing as they stumbled through the front door, and then the music would go on. We were often kept awake all night, which meant that we began to miss school and that I became permanently exhausted and close to despair through lack of sleep.

The men my mother brought home were all dossers who'd just come out of or were just about to go to prison for fraud, theft and violent crimes. There were few women amongst her new friends, but almost all the women who did come to the house had also spent time in prison – mostly for arson or violence, or both – and they were all even more mentally unstable than my mother.

It was difficult trying to get back to sleep knowing that people like that were partying in the house below me. Often, someone would push open my bedroom door, and as they stood there trying to absorb the fact that it wasn't the bathroom, I'd lie in my bed, holding the covers tightly and pretending to be asleep while I prayed they'd turn around and walk out again. Then, the following morning, after an almost completely sleepless night, I'd get up and go to school, where I'd get into trouble for being late or for being too tired to concentrate on my lessons.

Quite apart from being kept awake, though, it was frightening to live in a house full of volatile, threatening people who were always drunk or hung-over and whose constant presence forced me further into the protective shell I'd been building around myself for so many years of my childhood. But perhaps one of the worst – and I suppose inevitable – aspects of living in a house with so many thieves and drifters was that every single possession my grandparents had ever given me, including some treasured bits of jewellery, was either stolen (when my mother's friends were sober) or smashed up (when they were drunk).

Sometimes, my brother and I complained to my mother about one of her drunken, aggressive boyfriends, although the result was always the same. Instead of understanding why two young children might be afraid, she'd fly into a rage and shout at us, in her usual melo-dramatic way, 'You're nothing but selfish fucking bastards. You're going to leave home and then I'll be all on my own. But what would you care about that? You just want to bang another nail in my coffin; you're not worried about what'll happen to me when you've gone.'

She was always immediately furious if anyone questioned her right to do whatever she wanted. But, at the same time, she loved to have an excuse to make a big drama out of something and to reinforce to herself how hard her life was. The bottom line, though, was that it made no difference to her what we thought about anything. So our house became the local doss house for anyone and everyone to use and abuse in any way they saw fit. The only price they had to pay was to buy drink for my mother.

Every day, I'd come home from school, open the front door – if it hadn't already been left wide open as an invitation to any drunk who might want to join the party – and feel every tight, anxious muscle in my body begin to twitch. Almost every day there'd be people lying around, drinking and waiting for the pub to open again at seven. I'd try to keep out of the way until they left; but then they'd be back again a few hours later, invading my home and treating me like dirt.

Every morning, when I woke up from a nervous, fitful sleep, the house would be wrecked. There'd be bodies strewn across the debris as my mother's 'friends' slept off the effects of the enormous amounts of alcohol they'd consumed during the night. Then, when they woke up, they'd start the whole process all over again.

As soon as I got home from school, I'd go into the

kitchen and look for something to cook for dinner for myself and Chris, although it was often difficult to find anything to make a meal out of, after all the hung-over drunks had ransacked the cupboards looking for things to eat. First, though, I'd collect up all the empty bottles and dirty dishes that were strewn throughout the house, put the plates in the kitchen sink to try to soften and soak off some of the congealed food, and then scrub them until I'd nearly scrubbed off the yellow and blue lines that decorated their edges.

Part of my obsession with cleaning involved scrubbing almost every flat surface in the house with bleach, as I tried to wash away the visible dirt as well as disinfect the lingering contaminants that couldn't be seen. We had no washing machine, so on Friday evenings, as my mother and her friends were laughing and falling over each other in their haste to get out of the house and back to the bar, I'd fill a plastic bowl with water and wash my own and my brother's school clothes by hand. Then I'd pick up all the damp, foul-smelling towels that had been dropped in every room and carry them to the house of a neighbour, who I'd pay 50p to wash them in her machine.

It took me hours to restore some sort of order to the chaotic, filthy mess left in the wake of my mother and her friends. And almost as soon as I'd finished, the front door would burst open and they'd erupt into the hallway, clutching their bottles.

Ironically, because of my obsessive cleaning, my mother gained a reputation for keeping the house spotless. People would often tell me how great she was, and the drunks she brought home with her from the pub would sometimes look around them in awe and say, 'She keeps everything so clean you could eat your dinner off the floor.' Then they'd drop an arm across my shoulders and lean heavily on me as they added, through a haze of alcohol-induced emotion, 'She's a wonderful woman.'

I cleaned the house in the way I did not only because I was trying to avoid suffering from a constant stomach upset – or worse. I was also trying to exert some control in my otherwise completely chaotic life. Even so, it was irritating to have to listen to people praise my mother's (non-existent) housekeeping abilities, when the truth was that if it had been left to her, we'd all have been buried long ago under an avalanche of empty bottles and dirty glasses and plates. As usual, though, I said nothing.

As well as the itinerant drunks who slept, drank and fought in our house, we had countless lodgers. Anyone who told my mother they were homeless was allowed to move in and take one of our bedrooms, as long as the social paid their rent to her. It was usually my mother's bedroom that was let out, which made sense as she was up all night drinking and would then fall asleep on the sofa anyway. Sometimes, though, she rented out my brother's room and he'd sleep on the floor of mine, or on the end of my bed. And, although she didn't actually let out my room, I'd often find some drunk in my bed, waiting for me and expecting me to sleep there next to them.

Occasionally, my mother would take me to the pub with her, and it was there that I became friends with a girl called Sal and her sister. Sal's family was large; as well as Sal's mum, who was a friend of my mother, there was an alcoholic father and seven kids, and they all lived together in a horrible, dirty house – almost as filthy as ours used to be when I was younger and Carl lived with us. Also just like us, Sal's family seemed to have no money. The children's clothes all came from jumble sales, and their mother cut their hair herself – apparently, judging by the results, with pinking shears and her eyes shut. Sal and her sisters and brothers were really deprived – even by our standards – and it was when I was out in the town with Sal one day that we started shoplifting.

The first time, we stole some make-up, but as we got bolder we took clothes too. I knew my mother wouldn't notice that I had something new; she barely noticed me at all, and she never looked at me long enough to absorb any details, such as what I was wearing. As well as clothes to wear when we went out on the town, Sal also stole rubbers and pencils and anything else she needed for school, because she had, quite literally, nothing.

Then, one day when I met up with Sal, she told me that her mum had been going through the drawers in her bedroom and had found some of the things she'd stolen.

'I'm in deep shit,' she said. 'And I'm really sorry but my mum's going to speak to your mum. So you better watch out.'

I just shrugged and told her, 'I won't be in trouble. My mum won't care.'

But, the next day, when my mother burst into my bedroom and told me we were going round to Sal's house, it seemed I might be wrong.

When we arrived, Sal's mother told her to go upstairs and bring down all the things she'd stolen. Sal just stood there for a moment, twisting her fingers nervously, and then she walked out of the room and returned a few minutes later almost completely hidden behind the tower of objects she was holding in her arms. As she dropped clothes, make-up, stationery, CDs, etc, on to the floor, she glanced anxiously at our mothers, who were both standing in almost identical poses, hands on hips and mouths wide open in astonishment. I looked from one to the other, and then at Sal, who was tugging ferociously at a strand of her hair and whose lips were quivering as though she was about to cry.

Suddenly, both women fell to their knees and began to scrabble through the pile, grabbing what they wanted and laughing excitedly.

'Did they have this in other sizes? Do they do it in blue?' my mother asked, holding a T-shirt up against herself.

Sal's mother jumped to her feet, and I saw Sal flinch, as if she was expecting a slap. But, instead, her mother began pushing aside dirty cups and searching through bits of paper on a small, stained plastic table that stood to one side of the door into the hallway. After a few moments, she waved a scrap of paper and the stub of a pencil triumphantly above her head and, turning to my mother, said, 'Write it down, Jude.' And the two women began to write a list of all the things they wanted us to steal for them next time we went into town.

Although I hadn't stolen from shops before I started shoplifting with Sal, it wasn't the first time I'd stolen something. Ever since my mother had started drinking at the community centre, I'd been stealing loo rolls from the toilets there, throwing them out of the window and then going round the side of the building to pick them up. One day, the cleaner saw me standing outside the bar waiting for my mum and she came up to me and said, apparently out of the blue, 'If I ever find out who's stealing all the loo rolls from the ladies' toilets, I'll go for them.' I knew she was warning me, but it didn't stop me; it just made me more careful, because my mother refused to buy loo paper, so it was the only way we were ever going to have any at home.

In fact, my mother had tried to get me to steal something for her when I was just seven years old. We were in the local butcher's shop, waiting to be served, when she suddenly turned away from the counter and muttered at me, 'When he's not looking, get a chicken from the freezer.' At first, I didn't understand what she meant. Why did I have to wait until the butcher wasn't looking? But then I realised she wanted me to steal one.

I could feel myself flushing red with embarrassment as I whispered back at her, 'I can't. No.'

She kept her mouth almost closed, barely moving her lips, as she hissed, 'Fucking do it!'

But I was too frightened, and afterwards she'd shouted at me in the street and called me a 'fucking stupid cry baby'.

So I suppose it was inevitable that, eventually, I'd lose both my fear and the remnants of the morality my grandparents had instilled in me, and I'd start stealing stuff myself.

I always expected I'd end up in prison when I grew up. My grandparents had taught me to be honest, but living with Carl and my mother had eroded any integrity I used to have, and I no longer knew the difference between right and wrong. I'd been hurt so many times that I didn't care if I hurt other people. If I ever told my mother someone was picking on me or had hit me, it wouldn't even cross her mind to be sympathetic. She'd just scream at me that I must go back out and hit them twice as hard.

'You have to show them you're tougher than they are. Then they won't ever hit you again,' she'd shout, as though it was *me* that had done something wrong.

Hitting back harder than you've been hit isn't advice most parents would give their children. But I think it's probably the only piece of advice my mother ever gave me.

It wasn't until years later, when I met a girl I used to know when we were children, that I found out that even the toughest girls on the estate were frightened of me. Apparently, even when we were quite young, if I ever went into a pub garden when the girl and her sister were there, I'd tell them to leave or I'd beat them up, and they'd scuttle away as fast as their little legs would carry them.

I DIDN'T KNOW where Carl lived after he left our house, and I didn't ever think about him at all, other than occasionally to comfort myself with the thought that, however miserable it might be to have to live in a house full of drunks and criminals you'd normally cross the road to avoid, at least *he* wasn't there any more. Apart from the occasional drunk bursting into my room in search of the toilet and frightening me half to death, no one came into my bedroom at night. And no one sexually abused me.

It seems, however, that Carl hadn't forgotten my mother, and when he heard that men were coming round to the house, he insisted on visiting her. To my surprise – and dismay – my mother agreed. It turned out, though, that she'd done so not because she wanted to see Carl again, but because she was delighted to have the chance to show him what a great time she was having without him.

She set a date for the visit and arranged for all her new friends to come to a party and meet him. If I'd thought she'd take any notice, I'd have begged her not to let him into the house. I couldn't understand why she'd want him back in her life, even for one evening. She must have known he'd never had her best interests at heart – otherwise he wouldn't have actively encouraged her to start drinking again after her father died, when it was clear that eventually, one way or another, alcohol was going to kill her. But she was determined to show off her new friends to him and to let him see just how wonderful her life had become since he'd left.

For me, though, just the thought of Carl being in our house again made me feel sick with anxiety. Even if he didn't touch me – and I knew by that time that I could fight him off if he tried – the image in my head of his old, yellow skin, straggly hair and horrible, stained teeth and the memory of the sour stench of his breath made me shudder with hatred and disgust.

The party was in full swung by the time he arrived. Everyone except me was in the kitchen – pouring alcohol down their throats as though their lives depended on it. I'd been feeling ill all day and had gone into the living room to watch television and be on my own. So I didn't hear him arrive. And I didn't know he was in the house until the door of the living room was pushed slowly open and I looked up to find him standing in the doorway.

'Hello, Anna,' he leered at me. I could feel the heat rising into my cheeks as he walked towards the chair I was sitting in. 'I hear you pierced your ears. That doesn't sound like something you should do yourself. Let's have a look.'

He knelt down beside me, and I turned my head away as he leaned forward to lift a lock of my hair. Then he began rubbing his other hand up and down my leg.

'Fuck off!' I shouted, hitting his hands away and trying to kick out at him.

Almost losing his balance, he grabbed the arm of the chair and glanced quickly towards the door as he got to his feet. Then he hissed nastily at me, 'Still a fucking cold little bitch, I see,' and left the room to join the others in the kitchen.

For the next hour or so, as everyone continued to drink, Carl's hostility and jealousy towards all the younger men at the party increased steadily, and he was still standing in the kitchen when I tried to slip past the open door unnoticed on my way to the toilet. Suddenly, without any warning, he grabbed a bottle from the table beside him and brought it crashing down on the head of the man standing next to him. Beer and shards of glass flew everywhere, and the man sank slowly to his knees before his body crumpled and hit the floor.

Everyone was taken by surprise and for a split-second no one reacted. Then Carl started lashing out with the jagged edge of a broken bottle and, within seconds, there was blood everywhere. People were screaming and panicking, slipping and sliding on the blood and spilt alcohol as they tried to squeeze en masse through the kitchen doorway.

Snatching up another bottle, Carl pushed through the terrified, hysterical mob into the hallway and shouted, 'Where are you, Judith, you fucking bitch? I'll kill you.'

My mother was in the living room, screaming like everyone else, although she was too drunk to understand what was really happening. At that moment, Chris came running down the stairs and together we half-lifted, half-dragged her into the hall and out of the front door.

Carl came out of the house after us, roaring like a wild animal as he forced his way through all the people who were trying to escape. The blood was pounding in my ears and I looked around for somewhere to hide. But it was too late; Carl was too close behind us.

'Come on, Mum,' I begged, tugging at her arm with one hand and pushing her from behind with the other as I tried to propel her in the direction of a neighbour's house. 'He's going to kill us all. Please, Mum, try to run.'

I turned to look back over my shoulder at Carl, who was still waving a broken bottle and shouting obscenities at us. Finally, the seriousness of our situation seemed to penetrate my mother's alcohol-befuddled mind and she began to try to run with us. But it was clear we weren't going to make it to safety before Carl caught up with us. And even if we did manage to reach our neighbour's house ahead of him, we'd have to wait until she'd opened the front door and let us in – assuming she hadn't already heard the uproar and locked and bolted it.

A sob caught in my throat. Why was everything always so difficult? I was only 11 years old, and it seemed that I constantly had to make instant, important decisions I wasn't equipped to make. At that moment, more than at any other time in my life, I knew I *had* to keep my nerve and do the right thing. But I felt a familiar sense of hopeless despair at the thought that, once again, I was in a dangerous situation that had arisen because of something my mother had done and over which I had absolutely no control.

Suddenly, there was a scream from behind us and we all turned to look. Carl had stopped running; he was bending forwards, clutching his face with both hands, the broken bottle smashed into shards of glass on the ground beside him. He began to make a horrible wailing sound, like a wild animal in pain, and as he moved his hands away from his face, we all gasped. In the light from a street lamp we could see that it was covered in blood. Later, we found out that he'd accidentally cut himself while swinging the bottle around his head. But all I knew then was that even the agony of a shredded face wouldn't be enough to prevent him carrying out his intention of killing us.

My mother laughed a loud, spiteful, humourless laugh and then began to shriek obscenities at Carl. She was standing looking back the way we'd come, her hands on her hips, taking little sideways steps to try to keep her balance. But we weren't safe yet.

'Run!' I shouted to my brother, and we grabbed our mother's arms again and dragged her the last few yards to our neighbour's house, while she continued to curse and taunt Carl over her shoulder.

A couple of minutes later, from the safety of our neighbour's living room, we watched as Carl stumbled back towards our house, stopping every few steps to shout abuse at my mother and to wipe the blood from his face on to his shirt. We were still watching, and my mother was still cursing, when a police van pulled up in the street and half a dozen policemen in riot gear stormed our house. A few remaining people staggered out into the garden and disappeared into the night, and then three policemen walked back out of the front door with Carl in handcuffs and bundled him into the back of the van.

We waited until its red tail lights had disappeared around the corner at the end of the road and then we went home. Exhausted, and shaken by having come so close to what had seemed to be the inevitability of our own deaths, Chris and I crept upstairs to our beds and tried to sleep.

That was the last time I ever saw Carl. He'd been the worst part of my miserable existence for five years, during which time he'd sexually abused me almost every single day. And now he'd gone, taking with him my childhood, my self-respect and the last remnants of my confidence. He'd scarred me with his abuse and left me vulnerable to any man who was looking for sex. By destroying my self-esteem, he'd made me think I wasn't good enough to achieve anything in my life, and I felt as though I was beneath everyone's contempt. I hated looking at my reflection in a mirror, because I hated the sight of myself;

I was convinced that my past was written on my face and that everyone could read it and would despise me.

For as long as I could remember, every time life became too difficult for my mother, she tried to kill herself. So I grew up thinking that was the ultimate option available to me, and I attempted suicide several times. But each time I failed, as I seemed destined to fail at everything I tried to do.

Carl had stolen my childhood, but, perhaps even more importantly, he'd robbed me of my future.

11

Losing hope

MY MOTHER WAS known – by reputation at least – to most people on the estate, and everyone assumed my brother and I were the same as she was. Few of our neighbours would speak to us, mostly because of the noise from all the parties, the fighting and the trouble caused by the low-lifes my mother invited to the house. She had lots of 'friends', but every single one of them was someone no one else would have anything to do with.

Living in our house was like watching the same play night after night, but with a different cast of characters each time, as some of my mother's friends disappeared to prison and others were released after serving their sentences and came to take their places. It was a chaotic play, though, and it was punctuated by the sound effects of smashing glass and the screech of sirens as fights broke out and the police pulled up outside the house in cars and riot vans to break up drunken brawls or arrest someone who'd committed a robbery or some other act of violence elsewhere.

By this time, the years of heavy drinking and taking pills had destroyed my mother's prettiness, and she'd become old-looking and bloated. Despite the state she was in, though, she remained convinced that all the women she came into contact with were jealous of her. And it was partly as a result of this misconception that she had few female friends, and that all the ones she did have were alcoholics, just like her. Most of the women who came to the house came with the men, who'd picked them up for sex, and there'd often be several people having sex in the same room at the same time. Consequently, as well as being the first place you'd visit if you were looking for a small-time local criminal, our house also became known to the neighbours as the local whorehouse.

In the midst of the chaos, I kept on fighting my constant, never-ending battle against the squalor that threatened to overwhelm us. Then, one day, I came home from school to find the downstairs rooms of the house almost completely empty of furniture. Everything was gone, including the couple of stained, threadbare carpets that had provided two small, splinter-free islands on the wooden floors. At first, I thought we'd been burgled – my mother's friends had already taken almost everything else we owned, so why not the last bits of furniture too? But it turned out that everything had been gathered up and dumped in the garage to clear the house for a party. Afterwards, the furniture was never put back in place, so we lived without it, and sat on cushions on the living-room floor.

Life with my mother was as far away as you could get from the comfortable, well-ordered, secure life I'd lived for two years with my grandparents. We had absolutely nothing, and I felt as though that was what I was worth – nothing. Lots of our neighbours had very little, and lots of them were living lives that just a short time previously I'd have been ashamed to live myself. But now we had less than any of them.

I'd already given up hope that anything good was ever going to happen in my life. My mother didn't care about me, her friends treated me like dirt, and I felt worthless. Thanks largely to my mother's determination to drink herself to death, we'd descended the social scale until we were at the bottom of the bottom of the heap, and that was a situation no amount of bleach was ever going to change, although I kept on scrubbing and cleaning.

One day, when I was 13, I'd got off the school bus and was walking down the alley on my way home when I saw a boy just standing there, watching me. I'd become a hardened fighter by that time, and I wasn't usually afraid of people my own age, or even older. But the alleyway was narrow and secluded and it felt as though I was walking into a trap, although it had become a point of honour with me never to show any emotion, and I certainly wasn't going to give the boy the satisfaction of knowing I was afraid. So, although a shiver ran through my body and my palms were damp with sweat, I kept walking steadily towards him.

As I drew closer, I recognised him as a boy called Sam who went to my school and was a couple of years older than me. He had a vacant, drowsy expression on his face and a small, clear-plastic bag in one hand. As I passed him, he raised his other hand in an awkward salute and said, 'Hi.' I looked away without answering, and I could feel him watching me as I walked to the end of the alleyway and then turned the corner towards home.

He was there again the next day, and the day after that, and then, the fourth time I saw him, he reached out as I was passing, grabbed me by the arm and started kissing me. His breath had the sickly sweet, chemical smell of the glue he'd been sniffing, but I didn't turn my head away. And I didn't put up any resistance when he pulled me down the alley towards a small patch of litter-strewn scrubland behind the houses, where he pushed me down on to the ground. I didn't want to have sex with him, and I felt physically sick as I lay there while he tugged at my knickers, working them almost down to my knees before unzipping his trousers and doing what Carl had done to me so many times before.

I was worthless, nothing, so it didn't matter what happened to me, and it never even crossed my mind to say 'No'.

For the next few days, Sam waited for me in the alleyway every afternoon, and every day I let him do what he wanted. If we saw each other at school or anywhere else, he never spoke to me or acknowledged me in any way, and eventually something must have lit a small spark of resistance in my mind, because one day I decided to go home via a different route and avoid him. The following afternoon, he was waiting in the road near my house, but I walked past without looking at him. The same thing happened the day after that, and this time, when I'd been in the house for just a few minutes, the doorbell rang.

I was in the kitchen, and I could hear my mother sighing dramatically as she slammed her glass down on to the floor in the living room and stomped along the hallway to the front door. I heard her talking to someone, although I couldn't make out what she was saying, and then she giggled, in the embarrassingly girlish, flirty way she reserved for men, and called my name.

I stood in the kitchen doorway and looked towards the front door, where she was puffing cigarette smoke into Sam's leering, smirking face. She must have heard me behind her, because, without turning round, she said, in a horrible, coquettish tone, 'You didn't tell me you had such a handsome friend.' Then she turned to face me as she added impatiently, 'Don't just stand there, for God's sake,' and I could see she'd already lost interest in Sam.

I don't know why I went with him. I was feisty and cheeky at school, and often got into trouble for speaking my mind or for fighting when someone tried to bully me. In situations like the one with Sam, though, I seemed to become a different person, and it simply never crossed my mind to resist. So I went with him to the bit of wasteland behind the houses and had sex, and then I sat watching him as he adjusted his clothes and walked away without a word.

It was about a year since Carl had last abused me, and although the programme I'd seen on television had made me realise what he was doing to me, I'd never fully understood that I wasn't a virgin any more. Sam must have realised it, though, because he told his mates that we were having sex and that I was already a 'slag' and a 'whore' before the first time, which was a reputation that soon spread around both my school and the estate we lived on. I'm sure it was news that didn't come as a surprise to anyone who knew my mother, either person- ally or by reputation. But it wasn't really a fair condemnation of me, because I'd never wanted to have sex – not with Sam and not with Carl. In my mind, sex was something other people did to me; it had nothing to do with me as a person, and I simply didn't know it was something I might have had a choice about.

ALTHOUGH MY MOTHER still sometimes went to pubs, the bar at the community centre was really the centre of her life, and that's where she met her new boyfriend. Unsurprisingly, perhaps, Stevie was also an alcoholic, one of several brothers and sisters who all drank heavily and who all had violent, volatile reputations: whenever their names were mentioned as being involved in a fight in a pub or club in town, the police would turn up in riot gear. Some of them had teenage children who already had criminal records for violent assault, and one of them had been sent to prison for shooting and killing a young lad who inadvertently became involved in an attempt to rob a local store.

Stevie lived in lodgings a few streets away from ours and had a 16-year-old daughter who earned money as an escort. I didn't know what it meant and I used to wonder what or who might need to be escorted by someone like Margie, with her layers and layers of make-up and her tight skirts, although I think I guessed it might have something to do with prostitution.

At about five o'clock one morning, my mother decided to go and see where Stevie lived, and while she was walking along the street near his flat, she met his sister, Tina, who was pushing her newborn baby in a pram. Tina had the worst reputation of all of Stevie's brothers and sisters and she'd spent more of her adult life *in* prison than out of it. Her family used to joke that if she wasn't so crazy, she'd be in a mental hospital, and that she'd been thrown out of the last one she was in for frightening the other patients.

Unfortunately, after that first meeting, Tina and my mother became friends, and when they were both caught shoplifting, the police turned up at our house in riot gear to arrest them. Tina went wild, screaming, punching and kicking so violently that it took four policemen to restrain her. Before she was dragged out of the house and manhandled into the police van, she told me to take her baby to her parents' house, and, luckily, after she and my mother had been driven away, I managed to find someone who agreed to give me a lift there.

I was completely shocked by the state of the house Tina shared with her parents and some of her brothers and sisters. I thought our house was probably as dismal as any house could be, but this was in another league altogether. I'd never seen anything like it. The front door appeared to be made of cardboard – although I don't suppose they needed anything sturdier, as no one in their right mind would ever want to break *into* a house like that – and inside it was a filthy, disgusting, stinking dump. I felt awful leaving that poor baby there; it wasn't somewhere you'd have willingly left an animal.

Tina's mum had spent half her life in police stations and prisons waiting for her daughter, but this time I went with her to the police station to get Tina and my mother out. A few weeks later, when they were due to appear in court, they went into the courthouse toilets together as soon as they arrived, where they drank and giggled like a couple of stupid schoolgirls. They knew that the shop-keeper had failed to turn up as a witness – no sane person would have given evidence against Tina – and the case against them was duly dropped.

One day not long after that, my mother brought Tina back from the pub with her and they tried to feed the baby with a boiled egg. Even I could see that the poor little thing was far too tiny to be given solid food and, luckily, they soon lost interest and decided to leave the baby with me while they went out in search of more alcohol.

I had absolutely no idea how to look after a baby, but I was pretty sure she shouldn't smell the way she did. I lifted her thin, grubby, cotton nightdress and undid the sticky tape on her nappy. Then, using loo paper, I wiped off the worst of the horrible encrusted mess on her bottom before filling the basin in the bathroom with warm water and lifting her into it so that I could wash her red, chapped skin. Fortunately, there was a clean nappy in the bag Tina had dumped on the floor near the front door, and when the baby was comfortable and dry again, I put her in my bed, where she slept beside me for the rest of the night.

The next morning, Tina went home and told her mother she couldn't remember where she'd left the baby. Apparently, her mother was so upset she became almost hysterical, and when Tina finally did remember, she accused me of stealing her child! I knew it wasn't worth arguing with her, so I just caught the bus into town to hand the baby over. But it was no surprise when, not long afterwards, Tina's baby was taken into care and, shortly after that, Tina was found guilty of a horrific crime when she tried to kill someone who'd annoyed her, and would probably spend the rest of her life in prison.

Tina was just one of the many frightening, aggressive people my mother invited into our house. Her brother Stevie, who was my mother's new boyfriend, was even worse; he was probably the most volatile and violent of them all, and I was really afraid of him. But my mother didn't seem to have any idea of the danger she was putting me and my brother in – or perhaps she just didn't care.

It wasn't surprising our neighbours hated us. The noise from our house continued night after sleepless night and some of them, particularly the ones with young children, must have been driven close to despair. Almost every night a fight broke out about something, and every morning the house looked as though it had been ransacked. Sometimes, more damage than usual would be done and my mother would be furious. And then the same people would turn up the next evening clutching bottles of booze as peace offerings and muttering, 'Sorry, Jude,' and she'd let them in again.

Stevie and my mother hadn't been together long when his daughter, Margie, was thrown out by her mum and came to live with us as a lodger. She and her boyfriend took over Chris's bedroom, Chris slept on the floor of my room, and the social paid Margie's rent directly to my mother – a welcome contribution to her alcohol fund. So then all Margie's friends began turning up to party and doss at our house alongside all the other drunks and thieves my mother and Stevie brought home with them. And it was through Margie that I met and fell for Tony, an 18-year-old friend of her druggie boyfriend.

Whenever Tony came to the house, he talked and listened to me and it felt as though, almost for the first time in my life, someone really liked me. Over the last few years, I'd grown increasingly secretive and uncommunicative with almost everyone; I rarely told anyone anything unless I absolutely had to. But Tony asked me questions and seemed to be interested in my answers, and I told him about Sam, the boy who always lay in wait for me when I came home from school, and how I didn't want to have sex with Sam but I didn't know how to put a stop to it.

'He's just using you,' Tony told me. 'You've got to say "No", because if you don't, no one else is going to want you.'

As I'd been fairly certain for as long as I could remember that no one was ever going to want me anyway, the thought that they might was a completely new idea to me, and I was still turning it over in my mind when Tony smiled and said, 'I'll talk to him. Don't worry, Anna. I'll put a stop to it.' And in that moment I fell in love.

By the time I was 14, Tony had become my boyfriend, and had more or less moved in to the house. For the first time since I'd lived with my grandparents, someone seemed to want to have proper conversations with me, rather than using me purely as a sounding board for their drunken ramblings or as the target of their angry rants. It seemed too good to be true – which, of course, is exactly what it was.

For a while, I was happy in my belief that someone cared about me. In the end, though, it turned out that Tony was no different from any of the other users and abusers I came into contact with. He wasn't really interested in me or in anything I had to say. He was between girlfriends and I was a useful convenience for him – a source of regular sex and the means of obtaining a bed for the night whenever he needed one.

One night, when Tony was out and I was asleep, my bedroom door burst open. I woke up with my heart thumping and saw Carl walking towards me. Struggling to sit up, I raised my arms in front of my face in an automatic gesture of self-protection and shouted, 'Get out! Get away from me!' But the figure kept on coming until he was standing right beside my bed. Then he lifted the bedcovers, pushed me roughly against the wall and climbed in beside me. And it was at that point I realised it wasn't Carl: it was Margie's boyfriend.

I kicked out at him as hard as I could and hissed, 'Get out! What the fuck are you doing?' But he didn't answer. In fact, he didn't say anything at all; he just pinned my arms to the mattress and raped me. And then he got out of my bed and left my room.

Later, I discovered he'd gone back to the bed he shared with Margie and told her what had happened, explaining that he'd discovered she'd been sleeping with Tony and that he'd raped me as a means of getting back at her. I was shocked by what he'd done to me, and devastated when I realised how stupid I'd been to believe that Tony really cared about me.

I still thought I loved him, though, and I wanted our relationship to continue, despite what had happened. And then, one night when we were in my bedroom, my mother came home from the pub. She was drunk, as usual, but for once she hadn't brought anyone home with her. So there was no one to give her the attention she *had* to have, which I suppose is the reason she did what she did next.

I could hear her stumbling around downstairs for a while, and then the handle of my bedroom door turned slowly and she was standing in the doorway, swaying slightly and moving her head backwards and forwards as she tried to focus. Then, without a word, she walked across the floor to where Tony and I were sitting on the bed, took Tony by the hand, and led him out of the room.

I just sat there, speechless with shock, and watched as Tony stopped for a moment in the doorway, turned to grin at me and said, 'I've had the daughter, now I'm going to have the mother.' Then, when the door closed behind them, I lay down on the bed, wrapped a pillow around my head and cried myself to sleep.

I knew my mother was selfish and childlike in her need for attention and in her refusal to accept the fact that she couldn't have anything and everything she wanted regardless of the consequences, for her or for anyone else. But how could she – my own mother – have done such a terrible thing? How could she have taken from me the one thing she knew was really important to me?

After that night, Tony didn't bother coming back to the house. He told everyone what had happened, and when people asked me about it I tried to look indifferent as I told them it wasn't true. The hardest thing of all to have to face, though, was the fact that, after all the years of being alone and having no one to confide in, I'd finally allowed myself to open up to Tony, and he'd let me down.

It was a lesson I wasn't going to have to be taught again.

12

Accepting the inevitable

MY MOTHER OFTEN slept with the drunks she brought home with her, all of them disgusting old men and most of them married. She'd bring them into the living room when I was watching television and within seconds they'd be all over each other. One day, after having asked my mother and the man she was almost having sex with on the sofa to stop, I lost my temper and threw the TV remote control at them. I hadn't taken aim, but it hit the guy and he started shouting and swearing at me. Suddenly, my irritation evaporated and I just felt dejected and depressed, because it seemed as though I didn't deserve to have an opinion about anything. Whenever I said something my mother didn't like, she'd smack me around the face as hard as she could. So I'd learned mostly to suppress my resentment and anger, although every so often it would explode out of me and I'd start lashing out and hitting her back. What was even worse, though, was that, as well as not being allowed to have an opinion, I couldn't articulate the things I *did* feel strongly about; I simply didn't have the words to explain how I felt.

Even when my brother and I were little, my mother would often pick up someone in a pub and we'd all go back to his place, where Chris and I would be left alone downstairs to watch television, while my mother and some total stranger had sex upstairs. I suppose that's partly why I let men do whatever they wanted to me when I got older – I was just following my mother's example.

On one occasion, when I was in my teens, I was in bed when my mother came home with what sounded like several men. They went into the living room and I could hear them drinking and laughing, and then I heard my mother scream. I held my breath and listened, and she screamed again. She sounded really distressed, so I jumped out of bed and ran down the stairs. But I was too frightened to open the living-room door, and I was standing in the hallway, trying to summon up enough courage to turn the handle, when my mother burst out of the room crying. She was still sobbing as she told me that the men had become violent and had tried to pull her trousers off her, so that they could have sex with her. As soon as they saw me, though, they were apologetic, claiming, like naughty little boys, that it had been just a joke. Clearly, that wasn't true, but I managed to calm my mother down and dry her tears, and then I walked up the stairs with a sigh of despair as she went back into the living room and continued drinking with the men.

When I look back on my childhood now, it's no wonder I've suffered from depression almost all my life. I saw so many disgusting, sickening and depressing things when I was young that, by the time I grew up, I'd forgotten there were any nice things in life at all.

Not long after Tony left, we went to stay with my aunt for a weekend, and when we got back home again, the lodgers had had a party and the house was totally wrecked. Finally, my mother had had enough. She kicked Margie and her boyfriend out, and for the next few days they lived in a car parked right outside our front door. They sat there for hours on end, staring at our house and trying – successfully – to intimidate us, until eventually they moved on, as everyone did.

By the time I was in my early teens, my life was spiralling out of control. I was dressing like an adult, getting drunk every weekend at nightclubs and parties and then staying out all night – in fact, I was becoming just like my mother. For a while I thought I was having fun. I had no father to tell me what to do, and my mother was always too drunk to notice whether I was at home or not. So I did exactly what I wanted without anyone interfering, and it felt like freedom.

But although I might have appeared to be enjoying myself, in reality I was building up a store of so much pent-up anger that I'd erupt into sudden violence at the slightest provocation. I began to get into fights almost every day, and the headmistress at my school eventually threatened me with expulsion. When my behaviour became so bad that even my mother noticed and confronted me, I just laughed and said, 'Well, you got expelled at the same age. So I don't think you're in any position to say anything about it.'

Most of the men my mother brought home were losers, with almost as many problems as she had. Occasionally though, there'd be one who talked to me and was nice to me, and her new boyfriend Rickie was like that. Although he had a serious drinking problem, he was always kind to me and one day, after I'd nearly got expelled from school, he came into the kitchen when I was making tea, put his hand on my shoulder and said, 'Don't live your mother's life, Anna. You're worth more than that. You don't have to take the path she's taken.'

People rarely – if ever – spoke to me kindly, and I felt a lump come into my throat. I didn't think there was much I could do about how my life was turning out, but I appreciated the fact that Rickie seemed to care.

He patted my shoulder and said, 'Come on, love. Smile! I've never seen a child with such large, sad eyes.'

I tried to think of something to be happy about, but I couldn't. It seemed that every time I had something worth having – such as grandparents who loved me or a boyfriend who actually didn't – it was snatched away from me. Nothing good ever lasted. And, as if to prove the point, it wasn't long before Rickie moved away from the area to try to sort out his life.

My mother had long ago lost her job when her employer eventually tired of her returning drunk from her lunch break every day. So we were dependent on her weekly social security cheque, which – if we were lucky – arrived in the post on Mondays. Every weekend, she would spend every last remaining penny of her previous cheque on drink and, like a plague of locusts, the dossers would eat everything edible in the house. People often moan about not having any money, but I suspect few of them know what it's really like to have absolutely nothing, not even enough to buy a loaf of bread or a pint of milk. We'd already been blacklisted by the milkman, who'd been ripped off by my mother once too often, so he wouldn't let us have any milk unless we paid for it upfront.

I'd sit in the kitchen every Monday morning, watching and listening for the postman so that I could go to the front door and collect the brown envelopes as they dropped through the letterbox. Then I'd search through the pile of final warnings and reminders about unpaid bills until I found my mother's cheque from the social, which I'd take out and cash so that I could buy some food before she woke up.

I went to school only when I felt like it; when I didn't, I often went shoplifting so that I'd have the clothes and make-up I wanted and couldn't afford. I was drinking heavily and staying out all night, and then I started sniffing solvents.

One day, when I was 13, when a friend and I turned up at school in the afternoon to take an exam, we were so high that when our teacher told us off I became almost hysterical with laughter. Tears were streaming down my cheeks and I was doubled over, gasping for breath. The teacher must have thought I was choking, because she hit me on the back a couple of times. But then, when she realised I was laughing, she lost her temper and shouted at me, 'Get out of my classroom! I will not have you in here, disrupting everyone when they're trying to take an exam. Collect your things and go to the head's office immediately.'

Still helpless with laughter, I managed to walk out of the room. But instead of reporting to the headmistress, I continued walking – down the corridor, out of the main entrance and out through the school gates to catch the bus home.

I was banned from those lessons after that, and from some other classes, too, when my mother turned up at the school one day and threatened to hit a teacher who'd told me I was heading nowhere in my life.

I had no idea of right and wrong. It's a basic concept that children are supposed to learn from their parents. But what I was learning from my mother's example was to do exactly what I wanted to do and to ignore and despise anyone who criticised me or tried to moderate my behaviour.

On the days when I did go to school, I'd arrive in time for registration, go to just the lessons I was interested in, and then walk out of the gate and get the bus home again. From the time I was 14, I'd meet my mother in the pub every Friday lunchtime. It was the day her friend – my friend Sal's mother – got her money from the social, and Sal would often be there with them. Although the landlord of the pub knew my mother and would allow me to drink alcohol there in the evenings, he wouldn't serve me alcohol at lunchtimes. So, I'd have a few soft drinks and then, as it never seemed worth going back to school for the afternoon, Sal and I would go off together and disappear for the weekend.

Sometimes, we'd go to another pub at lunchtime, where the landlord must have assumed I was 18, because he served me alcohol without a second glance. And I suppose I did look much older than my age, because I'd dress up like a tart even when I was at school. I had several ear piercings and would wear make-up whenever I could get away with it, as well as shoes with stiletto heels, a tight skirt with a split in it and often a jeans jacket over my white school shirt and grey jumper. I was always being asked by teachers at school why I wasn't wearing the proper uniform and I'd just tell them, 'My mum can't afford to pay for it,' which, for some reason, they seemed to accept.

Sal and I were bad influences on each other, and while her mother blamed me for the trouble we were always getting into, my mother blamed Sal. From the age of 13, we were going to nightclubs and being served alcohol. There was never any shortage of men who were willing to pay for food and drink for us. And if we didn't fancy spending the evening with any of them, Sal would look around for a likely target and then disappear off into the toilets with him, returning a few minutes later with enough money to pay for at least a couple of drinks.

Most of the time, I was too drunk to know where I was or what I was doing, and Sal and I would often end up at houses with people much older than us, where we'd sit around taking drugs and drinking before walking home together in the early hours of the morning. Sal was more daring than I was, and more forward, and she'd often insist on hitching a lift, which I hated. One night, we were involved in a potentially serious crash when the drunken boy who'd picked us up swerved his mother's car off the road and hit a tree. But, even after that, we still took lifts from anyone who offered, and it's amazing we didn't come to any real harm.

Sal was a big, tough girl, who wasn't afraid of fighting anyone – male or female – and although she wasn't pretty, she never failed to pull men every time we went out. One night, when we were in a club, a man came over to chat to us. He was small and sleazy-looking and he started showing off, asking us to guess how much he'd paid for the heavy gold chain he was wearing around his neck.

'Let's have a look then,' Sal said, holding out her hand for the chain.

The man hesitated, and Sal let her arm fall to her side as she added, 'Well, it's all to do with the weight, isn't it? I thought that's what matters with gold.' Then she shrugged and turned away slightly, as if she didn't care one way or the other.

Immediately, the man lifted his hands to undo the clasp behind his neck, dropped the gold chain on to Sal's open palm and said with a smirk, 'Yeah, well, feel that then.'

Sal dug me in the ribs with her elbow, closed her hand over the chain, and we legged it out of the club.

Shortly afterwards, word got back to us that the man was going to contact the police if we didn't return the chain to him. And then we heard nothing more about it, until someone told us later that he'd discovered who we were and decided to cut his losses rather than risk the trouble everyone knew we could cause.

If anyone had asked, I'd have told them I was having a great time. In reality, though, I longed for someone to look after me. What I really wanted was someone who cared enough about me to lay down some rules and insist I got home at night by a certain time, and who'd be waiting for me when I walked through the front door. I was starved of affection, and although my mother was always greedy for attention herself, she never seemed to consider the possibility that I might need some too.

If my mother ever thought she was being ignored, or if she'd been unable to persuade anyone to come back to the house with her after the pub or bar closed, she'd go to bed and start wailing and crying so loudly she'd wake me up. She could keep it up for hours, until I eventually gave in and climbed into bed with her, and I can still remember the deep sense of humiliation I felt when she did it one night when I had a friend staying over. The noise my mother made was impossible to ignore; it sounded like the sobbing of a distraught child, and I was already awake when my friend was woken up by it and whispered to me, 'Anna, can you hear that? It sounds like someone's crying.'

'It's all right,' I whispered back through the darkness. 'It's just my mother. She does that sometimes. There's nothing really wrong with her. Go back to sleep.' Then I slipped out of my bed and went to my mother's room, leaving my friend to sleep alone for the rest of the night.

For some reason, my mother *needed* to be the centre of attention, and she often put herself – as well as my brother and me – at risk by inviting men into the house who most normal people would have refused to have anything to do with.

When I was taking my GCSEs and my brother had some end-of-year tests he wanted to do well in, we asked my mother if she could not have anyone round just for the week when we'd actually be taking our exams. She argued like a petulant child, and then, eventually, although still huffy and begrudging, she agreed. But as soon as someone knocked on the front door, she let them in, and we had to try to study to the accompaniment of loud music and drunken shouting.

One night, my mother and I were being driven back from the pub by friends and as we approached our house we could see cars parked outside. There were several men leaning against them, smoking and all clearly drunk, and I recognised some of them immediately as men who'd recently moved to a nearby travellers' site and had already earned themselves reputations for being extremely intimidating and violent.

'Don't stop,' I told the friend who was driving the car. 'Just keep going.'

I ducked down behind the front seat as I spoke, and tried to push my mother down with me. But she twisted her arm to shake off the grip of my hand and turned round to get a good look at the men out of the rear window as we drove past.

'Don't let them see us,' I told her, tugging at her sleeve urgently. 'Last time they came they trashed the house. If we wait round the corner for a few minutes, perhaps they'll give up and go away.'

However, my mother had seen that they were carrying bottles of alcohol, and she punched me hard on my arm as she shouted, 'Stop! Stop the car!' Then she jumped out while the wheels were still turning and ran back towards the house to let them in.

I had no alternative other than to follow her home, and as I stepped out of the car I could hear her laughing loudly. The men clustered around her while she fumbled to turn her key in the lock on our front door and then they swarmed into the house behind her.

I followed them and confronted my mother in the hallway.

'Chris and I don't want these people here,' I told her. 'They aren't even your friends. You barely know them. They're just using you so that they have somewhere to carry on drinking when the pubs close. Chris and I won't stay here tonight if you insist on having them here. You've got to make a choice between these people and your own children.'

She stood looking at me for a moment and then she shrugged her shoulders and said, 'You can both fuck off then. I choose my friends.'

So my brother and I stuffed some things into a couple of carrier bags and left to spend the night at a friend's house. But, when we got there, neither of us could sleep for worrying about our mother. Although we were used to our house being full of drunks and criminals, we knew that these men were different. They seemed to do everything together, like a pack of feral dogs, and when my mother had brought them home with her a few days previously, I'd felt that they were more frightening than even the worst of her usual friends.

After a couple of restless hours, tossing and turning and trying to sleep, I whispered to my brother, 'Chris, are you awake?' He answered immediately, and a few seconds later we were dressed again and walking back to our house to make sure our mother was all right.

We could see from several yards away that the front

door was wide open, and my heart was racing as we ran silently up the path. But the house was empty, except for our mother, who'd passed out on the sofa in the living room. The men had all gone, taking with them anything of even the smallest value.

I bent down and put my ear close to my mother's mouth to make sure she was breathing. Then we covered her with a blanket, locked the front door behind us and walked back to our friend's house, knowing that our mother would sleep through another night and wake up to another morning, which was the best we could ever hope for her.

Ever since I'd started going out to pubs, Chris was often left at home on his own in the evenings and, inevitably, he'd begun to look for other company. By the time he was 12 years old, he'd already been arrested several times for burglary and theft, and a year later he stopped going to school. Some of the men who drank at our house got him work on a building site and he started hanging round with them, drinking and taking drugs. And that's how his life continued for the next few years. He did try to make a new start when he was 16 by going to college, but he was kicked out for being rude and aggressive to a teacher, and after that he just drifted aimlessly in the company of various drunks and losers, looking for any outlet for his wild anger that presented itself.

One night, when he was 15, I came home and found him lying unconscious in his bed. He was covered in black vomit and when I touched him his skin was cold and clammy. I was certain he was dead and I was sobbing as I ran to the phone to call the doctor.

'I can't understand what you're saying,' the doctor kept telling me. 'Calm down and try to speak more slowly.'

But all I could say was, 'Please. It's Chris. Please come.'

And eventually the doctor understood. But he was furious when he arrived at the house.

'What kind of household is this?' he almost shouted at me. 'Your brother's drunk, as you clearly are too. He was this close...' He raised one of his hands and held his thumb and forefinger an inch apart, right in front of my face. 'This close,' he said again, 'to choking on his own vomit. A few minutes later and you'd have staggered home to find him already dead.'

I shrugged and turned away. It was a gesture intended to show the doctor that I didn't need or want his advice, although in reality I just didn't want him to see the tears that had rushed to fill my eyes.

For years, we put our neighbours through a living hell, and they must already have been close to breaking point by the time my mother made friends with a load of car thieves. At least half a dozen men used to turn up at our house every night after the pubs closed, shouting and laughing and waking up the entire neighbourhood. They stole cars to order, changing their number plates and parking them in the streets around our house while they waited to move them on. But everyone was too frightened of them – and of us – to complain.

None of the people who came to our house were our friends. They were all criminals and misfits who were happy to have found someone gullible enough to be of use to them. And as well as the ones we knew, we were always coming home to find men in the house we'd never seen before, men who'd heard through the grapevine that it was a good place to doss, or that my mother didn't mind – or even know – who she had sex with when she was drunk.

I came home from school one day to find her so drunk she wasn't even aware that there was a total stranger in the house. When I asked him to leave, he refused. So I pulled out an iron bar from behind the sofa and asked him again. It was a stupid thing to do, not least because he was clearly a lot stronger than I was. Fortunately, though, he left when I told him I'd called the police and that they were on their way to the house.

Whenever my mother went out, she'd latch on to people and follow them from one pub to another, and then ask them all back to our place at closing time. But whenever she needed help, not one of them would lift a finger for her. When she collapsed in a pub one day, her 'friends' simply moved on to another, leaving her unconscious on the floor, and the bar staff had to call an ambulance and then telephone my brother and me to let us know she'd been taken to hospital. Even then, she let them all into the house when they turned up a few days later.

I hated the way people treated her, and I was humiliated on her behalf by the fact that she didn't seem to care. It broke my heart that people thought it was all right to slag off my mother and say hurtful things about her, both behind her back and to her face. I suppose it was understandable because she did behave in a way that invited criticism, and I often had to go up to the pub or to a party at someone's house to bring her home when she was being a nuisance and could barely walk. She'd be sobbing and crying and I'd hear people making comments about how sorry they felt for me and how unfair it was that I had to deal with her. But they still took her money and served her with drinks. Even when she was so drunk she wasn't able to lift a glass to her mouth, there'd still be drinks lined up for her at the bar or beside her as she slumped over a table. She'd refuse to leave a pub if she knew she still had drinks to finish, and I'd sometimes put empty glasses under the table and tip her pints of lager into them when she wasn't looking so that she'd think she'd drunk them.

No one except Chris and me seemed to care that she was drinking herself into an early grave. Despite everything, we felt very protective towards her, which was something she was aware of and would often use to her advantage. She was very manipulative, and she knew we'd stick up for her if anyone upset her. She used to tell us that the other women at the club were jealous of her and that they hated her because they were afraid she'd steal their husbands. She claimed that there was one particular woman who often gave her a hard time, and one day she told us about some nasty things this woman had said to her, before adding innocently that 'the bitch has just got a new car'.

That night, I walked past the woman's house in the dark and scratched deep, ugly lines in the shining paint-work of her brand-new car with a key. The next day, my mother was over the moon when she heard the poor woman telling everyone what had happened and how she couldn't understand why anyone would want to do such a terrible, mean thing to her.

After that, my mother made a point of telling me whenever anyone upset her, knowing that I could be relied upon to harass and bully them. I was playing a role she had created for me; it was a role I didn't really want to play, but I couldn't see any way of escaping from it.

Every Saturday, I worked in a local garden centre. It was a small place, with just two other members of staff, and we took the money in a building that was really nothing more than a large shed. I was working alone in there at the till one Saturday morning and had just finished serving a customer when I noticed two men standing near the door. Although neither of them seemed to be looking at me, I had the feeling I was being watched. One of them was slowly turning a revolving rack of gardening books and the other had picked up a plastic container of something and appeared to be studying its label intently.

As the customer I'd been serving left the shed, one of the men stepped forward to hold the door open for her, and at that moment the other man approached me at the counter.

'Are you Anna?' he asked me. 'Jude's girl?'

'Maybe,' I said warily, hoping my voice portrayed a nonchalance I certainly wasn't feeling. 'Who's asking?'

'We hear you're going to stab us in the back,' he sneered, leaning across the counter and breathing stale cigarette breath into my face.

'And why would I want to do that?' I asked, glancing towards the door and realising that the man standing watching us was his mate.

'Apparently, we upset your mum, and she's telling everyone you're going to come after us when we're not looking.'

If I hadn't been so frightened, I might have laughed at what, in different circumstances, would have seemed like some sort of schoolyard stand-off. But this was infinitely more dangerous, and I knew that the only way to deal with it was to try to get the men on my side.

'I don't know anything about you,' I told him. I laid my upturned hands on the counter in a gesture of openness and shrugged as I added, 'You don't want to take any notice of anything my mum says. She lives in a world of her own. Besides, do I look stupid enough to come after a couple of blokes twice my size?' I made a squeaky sound that was supposed to be a self-deprecating laugh.

'Glad to know you've got more sense than your mum.' The man took a step backwards, and I released the breath I hadn't noticed I'd been holding. 'Let's just keep it that way, shall we?' He turned away from me and his mate opened the door of the shed.

It wasn't the first – or the last – time my mother put me in a dangerous, potentially life-threatening situation. Although I could be aggressive and would sometimes retaliate when she told me that someone had upset her, I didn't really want to fight with anyone. But because of what my mother told people about me, I was earning a reputation I didn't wholly deserve and certainly didn't want. I knew there was no point trying to explain that to her, though, because she simply did whatever she wanted, despite the consequences, and the possibility that a couple of men might beat up her daughter because of something she'd said would not have stopped her.

After my grandfather died and my grandparents' house was sold, there was some money to be shared amongst their children, and when one of my uncles told my mother he was going to hold on to her share for her, because he knew she'd only blow it on drink, she was furious. She screamed and threatened and accused her brother of stealing her money, and then she had the bright idea of making me lie to him by telling him she needed it to do up the house. I'm ashamed to say that I must have been a convincing liar, because he *did* hand the money over to my mother and, as he'd predicted, she *did* blow the whole lot within a few weeks. The only thing she bought for the house was a new stereo system for her parties. The rest she spent on booze – drawing £100 out of the bank every day for several days on her way to the pub – or gave as 'loans' to people who had no possible means, or intention, of ever paying her back.

One of the car thieves came up with a scam and she was immediately suckered in. He persuaded her to write a cheque in his name, explaining that he would cash it and then she could report it stolen and cancel it, so that the bank would end up paying out on it twice. But, of course, as the car thief knew would happen, the bank didn't reimburse her when she reported the cheque stolen *after* it had been cashed and cleared through her account. So she lost that money, too.

Then another two men got her to lend them some money to start up a business. What it actually involved was them using the money she gave them to open bank accounts in false names and then writing cheques for money they didn't have to buy various expensive items they then sold. Unfortunately, though, they were already known to the police – and clearly weren't very bright – and the false names they used were so close to their own that it wasn't long before there was a knock at our front door a few minutes after they'd arrived at our house one day, and they were arrested and subsequently convicted of fraud.

Within a few weeks, my mother had lost every penny of her inheritance from my grandfather – as my uncle had known she would – and nothing in our lives had changed. It was time for me to stop hoping that things one day might be different, and to accept my life as it was, and as it was always going to be.

13
Guilt, remorse and unfounded optimism

ALTHOUGH I'VE SUFFERED from crippling depression since I was in my teens – or maybe even before that – I always refused to ask the doctor for medication. Because that would have meant I was just like my mother. I loved her, despite everything, but being *like* her was the very last thing in the world I wanted.

By the time I was 14, the truant officer had become a regular visitor at our house, and on one occasion she arrived on a Friday evening, just as I was getting ready to go out. I opened the front door and she followed me into the hallway, where I continued to plaster make-up on to my face.

'Why weren't you in school today, Anna?' she asked me, in a voice which gave away the fact that she didn't really expect me to give her a sensible answer.

'I'm ill,' I told her rudely, adjusting my mini-skirt and

sliding my feet into a pair of bright red shoes with five-inch heels.

The truant officer sighed. It was clear that she was weary of trying to cajole me and my mother and of threatening us with dire warnings about what would happen if I didn't attend school. So she tried a different tactic and began to explain why going to school was important for me, personally. I stood with my back to her, barely listening, until she seemed to have run out of ideas and ended lamely with, 'If you don't go to school, you won't have any friends.'

I spun round at last and laughed in her face. Where the hell did she think I'd been all day? I'd been out with my friends, all of whom came from backgrounds similar to – although perhaps not quite as extreme as – my own and all of whom bunked off school just like I did. I felt a rush of superiority and scorn for this dowdy, middle-aged woman who clearly had little, if any, fun in her life and who would probably benefit enormously from a night out like the one I was about to have. I gave a short, nasty laugh and turned my back on her again, and finally she gave up. With one last warning to think about the consequences of my actions, she opened the front door and left, and a few minutes later I click-clacked my way along the pavement after her.

In reality, my bravado was all a sham. I wasn't enjoying

myself. It was true that I had lots of friends, but I was deeply unhappy and lonely, and I'd often sit on my own in my bedroom and scratch deep lines into my skin with a needle, until it looked as though my arms had been slashed with a knife. Every night, I lay in my bed and prayed I wouldn't wake up in the morning. And every morning I cried with self-pity and exhausted despair when I opened my eyes and found I was still alive and facing another miserable, pointless day.

As children, we never had a curfew on what time we could come home at night; we went out when we wanted, and we came home when – and if – we wanted. We were very much street kids. Even when we were little, we'd always be out long after all our friends had gone home. There was nothing for us to go home for, because there'd be no food in the house, and our mother would either be out or too drunk to know what was going on. So, from the age of 13, I was totally out of control – getting drunk, stealing, bullying and going to all-night parties and clubs.

Only twice throughout all the years I lived at home did my mother ever come looking for me. The first time was when I was 14 and she was dragged out of the house in the early hours of the morning by the mother of the friend I was with. We'd broken into the cellar of the community centre and had stolen crates of alcohol, and when my friend's brother found us, we were drinking with some older kids in the local park. As we walked along the road with him, we saw our mothers coming towards us. My friend's mother was furious, and as soon as we were within arm's reach, she smacked my friend round the head and told her she was grounded for a month. My mother didn't say anything, though, and I knew that the thought of grounding me would never have entered her mind. She didn't really care where I went and who I went with, and she certainly wasn't about to curtail her own social activities by having to stay at home and check up on me. But when I glanced at her face, I was amazed to see that she was fuming too – although it turned out that what *she* was cross about was the fact that she'd been at home in bed with some man she'd just met at the pub when my friend's mother had banged on the door and insisted they should go out and look for us.

The second, and last, time she came searching for me was not long afterwards, when I had gone out with a friend and her younger sister. We'd been in various pubs around town and when our mothers found us, it was very late at night and we were walking along the street about four miles from home. Although my friend's mum was drunk, she was driving her car, and they pulled up beside us and shouted at us to get in. The night ended with the car breaking down and all of us having to walk home in the pouring rain, screaming and shouting at each other, which I'm sure simply confirmed to my mother that it was far better just to let me get on with doing whatever I wanted to do.

I tried to convince myself I was having a great time and that I was lucky not to have anyone interfering. I even told myself that the crushing despair I felt whenever I was alone was just part of being a teenager – it was my hormones; every teenager felt the same. In reality, though, I knew that my life was as miserable and as empty as it was possible for it to be, which is probably why, when I was 15, I decided to try to find my father. Nothing had been able to fill the void that had been inside me for as long as I could remember, but perhaps my father could.

As soon as it occurred to me, the thought of finding my father became an obsession. Although I'd hated him for years, I became convinced that it would make everything in my life better and that I'd be happy. By this time, my grandmother had several other grandchildren, who she spent time with, and it seemed I had lost the special place I used to have in her heart. She and my aunts disapproved strongly of the way my mother was living, and they only ever came to our house when they absolutely had to, and then stayed for as short a time as possible. I felt as though they'd all abandoned me, although I realise now that they must have felt *I'd* turned against *them*, as I'd become increasingly unresponsive and surly in my attitude towards them. Whatever the reason, the result was that there was no one in my life who seemed to care about me, and no one I could turn to when the loneliness and depression threatened to overwhelm me.

Now I hoped that was all about to change – as soon as I found my father.

I did some research and over the next year wrote to every organisation that might possibly be able to help me in my search. Unfortunately, it turned out that he wasn't on the electoral roll, and one after another the replies came back saying, 'Sorry, we can't help you.' With each letter I received, a bit more of my excited optimism turned to frustrated disappointment, and then to even deeper depression. Even so, I was determined not to give up until I'd tried everything. And that was when I had a bright idea, and in my school lunch hour one day went to the local library and made a list of all the people in the area where I'd been born who had my father's surname. We didn't have a phone at home, so I had to persuade friends to phone each number on my list and ask to speak to Paul Lowe.

Bizarrely, one lady told my friend that that was the name of her dog – which, at the time, seemed about as close as I was going to get. But then the man who answered another phone call on another day turned out to be my father's brother. He gave my friend my father's phone number and she wrote it down on a scrap of paper. For the next couple of days, I carried it round with me everywhere, unfolding and refolding the paper again so many times that it began to disintegrate. It wouldn't have mattered if it had though, because although I liked looking at the numbers that were written on it in blue felt-tip pen, I'd memorised them and can still remember them to this day.

Eventually, I plucked up the courage to phone my father from my friend's house, by which time his brother had warned him and he was expecting my call.

'Dad?' I could hear the anxiety in my voice. 'It's Anna…your daughter.' I sat down abruptly on the stool beside the telephone table.

'What do you want?' he snapped.

They were the first words my father had spoken to me in almost ten years and they bore no relation to any of the words I'd imagined him saying during the months when I was searching for him.

'I don't want anything,' I answered, trying not to sound hurt or – something I knew would be even worse in my father's eyes – critical. 'I just wanted to find you. I thought you might like to see me.'

'Where's your brother? I'd like to see *him*.'

Suddenly I remembered the sneering tone my father always used to have in his voice whenever he spoke to me. I felt the sting of tears in my eyes and I tried to comfort myself with the thought that at least he hadn't put the phone down, and he was saying *something*. I told him Chris was fine and that he was doing well at school.

'I'm getting married in a couple of months,' my father interrupted. 'You can come to the wedding if you want to.'

'Both of us?' I asked, not waiting for the answer before I almost shouted, 'Oh Dad! That would be great!'

My heart was thumping with excitement and pleasure. My father had asked me to his wedding. That must mean he did care about me after all. It was probably just that he didn't know how to express his feelings – which was something I knew about only too well.

We arranged to meet – my brother, my father and me – at a pub a couple of weeks later. I couldn't wait to get home and tell my mother the good news. I hadn't told her I'd been looking for my father, and now I was so wrapped up in the triumph of having found him that I didn't anticipate her reaction. Before I'd even finished relating to her what my father had said – leaving out the fact that he'd clearly been more interested in my brother than in me – she'd burst into tears and run upstairs, where the sound of sobbing and wailing could be heard from the other side of the bedroom door she'd slammed behind her.

The reactions of my grandmother, aunts and uncles were equally negative, although considerably less emotional than my mother's.

'I can't believe you've done this,' one of my aunts told me. 'How *could* you have gone behind our backs like this? After all we've done for you. Your grandmother is so hurt and disappointed. We've kept you away from your father all these years because of the way he treated you. Didn't you think you owed it to us to be honest and open about what you were doing?'

I was sure that my mother's family were just jealous because I'd found my father, and that they were afraid they might lose me if he decided he wanted me to go and live with him and his new wife. Although that didn't really seem like a realistic possibility, having managed to track him down against all the odds, I was prepared to believe that no miracle was too unlikely to be impossible. No one seemed to be able to understand the overwhelming need I had to meet my father, and I despised them for their lack of support for me and for their whingeing complaints about being hurt and disappointed. Couldn't they see that I *deserved* to have a dad just like everyone else, just like their own children.

A few days before the scheduled meeting with my father, there was a family party at the house of one of my aunts. I was still upset with them all for their refusal to understand how I felt, and I didn't really want to go. But my mother insisted – although I couldn't understand why, as it was bound to end in arguments, just like all family occasions that included my mother.

My grandmother was due to have an operation the following day, and despite the fact that when I arrived she looked pale and was clearly in pain, I wanted everyone to feel the same hurt that I was feeling and I was determined to pay her back by ignoring her. So I refused to kiss her and I barely spoke to her. I was cocky and smugly indifferent to everyone's anger and disappointment. I'd found my father despite their attempts to stop me making contact with him, and I blamed them for keeping me away from him for so long.

I had convinced myself that my life would have been very different if my father had been a part of it, and if my mother's family hadn't done their best to stop me seeing him. In fact, that was all a fantasy, but it was a more palatable explanation than the real one – that they had been trying to protect me from a father who'd never even attempted to see me because he had absolutely no interest in me or in my well-being.

On the night of the family party, my grandmother went up to bed early, and I left the house without so much as a 'goodbye'.

The next day, I walked out of school at lunchtime and

went up to the pub to meet my mother as usual. But she wasn't there, and I knew immediately that something bad had happened. I walked back to school trying not to think about all the different, equally terrible, possibilities, and arrived just as my uncle drew up outside the gates in his car.

I stopped and waited while he turned off the engine, got out of the car and strode towards me, putting his hand on my shoulder as he asked, 'Do you know why I'm here?' I nodded and burst into tears, because I could tell from his face that my grandmother had died.

I didn't go to her funeral; I didn't think I deserved to. I'd loved my grandmother more than anyone on earth, and she'd loved me. For two years she'd taken care of me and shown me what a good life was like. And on the very last day of *her* life, I'd hurt her by shrugging off her attempt to put her arms around me. Her death was *my* fault, because I deserved to lose her. But she hadn't deserved to die. I was overwhelmed with guilt and by an almost physically painful sense of loss. I knew that if God could hear my thoughts he'd strike me down, but even so I couldn't help wishing that it had been my mother who'd died that day and not my beloved grandmother.

A few days later, Chris and I were sitting in a pub, at a table near the door, waiting for my father to arrive.

My emotions were still in turmoil, and I wasn't sure whether the sick sensation in the pit of my stomach was grief, excitement or anxious anticipation. My mother had insisted on coming with us, and she was standing nervously at the bar, her eyes flicking repeatedly towards the door, but never once looking in our direction.

My grandmother's death on the operating table at the local hospital and the guilt I felt about my attitude towards her just hours before she died had sapped the last remnants of my confidence and sense of self-worth. It seemed that bad things were always going to happen to me and that they were all I really deserved, and I began to be afraid that meeting my father might prove to be just another one of them.

There was a constant stream of people coming and going in the pub, and I examined all of them closely. Then the door was pushed open by a small, dark-haired man, who glanced around him before striding up to the bar. I didn't recognise him, and although he looked directly at us, he didn't recognise my brother and me either. So it was only when my mother greeted him that I realised he was my father. They stood together awkwardly for a moment while he bought himself a drink, and then he came and sat at our table, his back turned slightly towards me as he greeted Chris. It was clear immediately that he had no interest in me, and when he started running down my grandmother and blaming everyone but himself for everything that had happened to tear our family apart, I realised with a sickening sense of disappointment that everything everyone had ever said about him was true. He was a nasty, selfish, self-centred, irresponsible man who cared nothing for anyone but himself. I couldn't imagine why he would be getting married, as it seemed unlikely he had the capacity to love anyone.

When we left the pub that day, I went home, sat in my bedroom and cried. Because I'd insisted on tracking down my father, my grandmother had died thinking I hated her. She'd looked after me and loved me since the day I was born, and I'd hurt her by kicking her when she was down – and all because of that man.

I realise now that although she hadn't understood my attitude at the time, or why I'd stopped confiding in her and even really talking to her at all, she'd still loved me. I just hope she's watching over me somewhere and knows that I loved her too, and that I was so hurt and damaged by the abuse I'd suffered and the life I'd been living that I simply couldn't help myself.

At the time though, I became very depressed. One evening, I left my friends at a club and started walking home alone in the dark. I was like a zombie, so overloaded with confused emotions that I'd switched off completely and was unable to feel anything. Apart from the two years when I'd lived with my grandparents, my life had always been full of fear and unhappiness, but I'd never felt as low as I did that day. All I could think about was my grandmother and how badly I'd let her down, and I decided I couldn't bear the thought of living a moment longer.

When I got home, I could hear my mother talking and laughing with someone in the living room. She was drunk, as usual, and probably wasn't even aware that I'd come into the house. I went upstairs, opened the door of her bedroom, took the lids off some of her many bottles of pills and started shoving handfuls of them into my mouth, gagging as they stuck in the back of my throat when I tried to swallow them. Then I left the room and walked across the landing to my bedroom, already in a state of near-collapse.

As I pushed open my bedroom door, I stumbled, crashing against the side of my bed as I fell. The noise was loud enough to bring my mother upstairs – which was something she was even more than usually reluctant to do when she had company. I was only dimly aware that she was in the room, and although I could hear her voice, I didn't understand what she was saying. She must have thought I was drunk, because she pushed me on to the bed, threw a cover over me and left the room, closing the door behind her.

My eyes wouldn't focus; everything seemed to be spinning slowly around in my head and I felt sick and heavy, as though my whole body was filled with lead. I remember thinking that I mustn't vomit, because that would bring up the tablets before they had a chance to get into my bloodstream. And then I must have passed out.

The next thing I remember was lying in bed thinking that being dead was just like being alive – until I opened my eyes and realised I wasn't dead at all. It seemed impossible to believe that the quantity of pills I'd taken hadn't killed me. Was nothing in my life ever going to go the way I wanted it to go? I began to sob and scream hysterically, punching myself, tearing at my hair and ripping my skin with my fingernails. Other people managed to kill themselves, so why couldn't I? What was wrong with me? I hated my life and all I wanted was to die. But I couldn't even get that right. No wonder my father didn't like me and my mother didn't care enough about me to stop drinking and try to be a proper mother to me. I wanted to hurt myself, to punish myself for failing and for being so useless at everything I tried to do.

I had no one to talk to, no one to confide in, and throughout the rest of that day I felt terrible – ill and weak and desperate. Later, in the afternoon, my mother confronted me, demanding to know if I'd taken her pills, but I denied it, and she never mentioned the subject again.

THE DAY BEFORE the wedding, my father took my brother out, bought him lunch at the pub and spent a small fortune on a new outfit for him. But he had no such interest in me; he simply gave his fiancée £10 and told her to get me a dress. That night, my brother and I slept at his flat, until we were woken up in the early hours of the morning by my father and his friends bursting into the bedroom we were sharing.

'You disgust me,' my father shouted at me, his voice slurred by drink. He flicked the light switch and I raised my hand to shade the glare from my eyes. 'You couldn't even be bothered to phone me yourself,' he yelled. 'You had to get your friend to do it for you. Or maybe that was because you just didn't have the guts.'

'Yeah,' one his friends leered over my father's shoulder, and I pulled the covers up to my chin, hoping no one could see the fear in my eyes.

'You're just like your no-good, worthless whore of a mother,' my father shrieked, breathing alcohol into my face as he leaned down towards me and steadied himself with one hand on the edge of my bed.

'Yeah,' his friend chorused again, waving his finger in the air to emphasise his support.

I felt tears pricking my eyes and had to swallow hard to stop them spilling out on to my pillow. I was gutted by my father's accusations, but I was determined not to let him or his drunken friends see how hurt and shocked I was.

The next day, at the wedding reception, my father introduced my brother to everyone, but ignored me completely. Although I tried to talk to his family, they barely acknowledged me. One of his brothers looked me up and down with an expression of open dislike and said, 'I didn't even know Paul had any kids.' I sat for a while next to his mother – now, my only grandmother – but she didn't address a single word to me directly, and after a while I went to sit with my new stepmother's parents, who, in stark contrast to the members of my own family, were kind and pleasant to me.

Nothing had changed. My father was glad to have made contact again with my brother, but it seemed that he disliked me as much as he'd ever done. I didn't know that his attitude was, at least in part, due to the fact that he hated women. I thought it was my fault, that there was something about me specifically he disliked, and I wondered how I'd let myself hope and believe things might work out differently. I'd almost convinced myself that if only he got to know me, he'd realise he loved me after all. It had been a stupid idea, doomed to certain failure, as there was clearly nothing lovable about me.

In the end, by tracking down my father, all I'd managed to achieve was to hurt my grandmother on the day before she died and to make my father hate me even more than he'd done before.

14

Desperate for love

I WAS 16 and my life was in chaos. The one person in the world who cared about me – apart from my brother, who was too young to do anything to help me – had died, and my attempts to forge a link with my father had ended in dismal failure, leaving me more lonely and depressed than I'd been before. So I suppose it wasn't really surprising that I hooked up with the first person who showed me any sort of affection.

Tyrone was 20, an illiterate drifter who travelled round the country with members of his family and a constantly changing group of friends, living in squats. He told me that our house was one of the first 'proper homes' he'd ever stayed in – which just goes to show what sort of places he was used to, as most people wouldn't have used those words to describe our damp, dismal, sparsely furnished, prefab council house. When he asked me out, I agreed to go, despite all the things I knew about him, and shortly after that, he moved in to live with me.

It was clear from the first time his family met me that they hated me. And my family hated him. He'd already served a prison sentence, and when we met he was waiting to go to court for another violent crime he'd committed. They were facts that didn't mean anything to me, though – almost everyone I knew was a criminal – and it wasn't long before I'd fallen in love with him and he told me he loved me, too. It was the first time anyone other than my grandparents had said that to me, and I really wanted to believe it.

It seems shocking to me now to think that my self-esteem had sunk so low that I was elated when a violent criminal told me he loved me. But I was walking on air. I'd sometimes imagined having someone of my own, someone who would look at me and see beyond my care-fully constructed, tough, don't-care facade, and who'd want to take care of me – although I'd never really expected it to happen.

After Tyrone moved into the house, there'd often be a knock at the front door in the early hours of the morning and his mates would troop into the living room, carrying metal bars. While they put on gloves and crash helmets, Tyrone would come up to the bedroom, kiss me and say goodbye, just as if he were going off to do a normal job.

Then he'd leave the house with his friends to do smash and grabs, while I lay in the darkness, waiting for him to come back and hoping he hadn't been arrested. It was usually around five o'clock in the morning when he sneaked back into the house, and when I woke up to get ready for school, he'd be fast asleep on the sofa.

Tyrone and I planned to move out of my mother's house and live somewhere together. I couldn't wait. The one thing I really wanted was to be able to make a home for myself where everything wasn't ruled by my mother's erratic, hysterical and often frightening behaviour, and where we weren't invaded every night by the loud, disgusting drunks, vagabonds and prostitutes she called her friends. How I managed to convince myself that having friends who were vicious itinerant criminals would be any better, I don't now remember. Perhaps it was because I only ever met people who were on the fringes of society for one reason or another, so it was simply a case of wanting to choose my own friends from amongst them, rather than having my mother's choices forced on me.

One morning, about an hour after Tyrone had left the house to get a taxi to take him the ten miles or so to where his family was staying, I was woken up by the sound of people talking under my open bedroom window. I flattened myself against the wall and gently lifted the edge of the curtain so that I could look out without being seen. A taxi and two police cars were parked on the road outside the house, and I could see a man and four policemen standing by the front door. As I watched, one of the policemen banged on the door with his fist and shouted, 'Police. Open up.'

The police turned up regularly at our house, but some sixth sense told me that this time their visit had something to do with Tyrone. I knew my mother would be in a deep, almost comatose sleep and that she wouldn't wake up, however hard and persistently they thumped on the door. And I certainly wasn't going to answer it, partly because I should have been at school – where I assumed my brother already was – and partly because I didn't want to risk saying or doing anything that might get Tyrone arrested.

I let the edge of the curtain drop back against the wall and climbed into bed, and eventually they left.

Later that day, when Tyrone came home, he told me what had happened. When he left our house that morning, he'd quite quickly found a taxi, and the taxi driver had agreed to take him to the address where his family and friends were staying. But when they arrived there and the taxi driver asked for his fare, Tyrone pulled out a knife and held it to the man's throat. It wouldn't have been a stretch of anyone's imagination to believe that Tyrone would slit their throat for the sake of a few pounds, so the taxi driver had quickly handed over his wad of money and Tyrone had run off. Unfortunately, though, when the taxi driver took the police to the street where he'd picked Tyrone up and they started asking questions, the neighbours probably fell over themselves in their eagerness to point them in the right direction.

I had absorbed at least some of my mother's belief that almost anything was justified in the pursuit of getting what you wanted, and I didn't think Tyrone had done anything wrong or feel any sympathy for the taxi driver, who must seriously have thought he was going to lose his life that day. I'd be appalled today if I heard someone had done such a terrible thing, but it didn't bother me at all at the time. My mother had taught me well: all that mattered in life was being able to do what you wanted to do, whether you could pay for it or not.

I refused to listen to what anyone said about Tyrone. Even his own family and friends told me he was crazy and that he was far more brutal and vicious than I realised. But I ignored them, just as I ignored the little voice in my head that warned me that my relationship with him would only end in tears. When I heard terrible stories about the things he'd done, I told myself they weren't true, or that he'd been involved only as an innocent bystander.

At some level, I must have known I was lying to myself, because whenever he was drunk – which was almost every night – he abused me, both mentally and physically. He'd often go out ram-raiding with his mates – reversing stolen cars into shop windows and stealing everything they could lay their hands on – and if I'd been out too and he got home before me, he'd fly into a rage, punching and kicking me and calling me a whore until, if I was lucky, my brother would burst into my bedroom to separate us.

Despite everything, though, I thought I loved Tyrone. My father had beaten my mother, and almost all my mother's boyfriends were aggressive and violent. So, in the context of the life I was living, there was nothing to remind me of what my grandparents had taught me about a completely different sort of love. Deep down, I think I must have known that what I felt for Tyrone wasn't love at all. But I was re-living my mother's life, and I didn't know how to break the pattern and stop myself becoming a victim, just like she was.

As well as abusing me physically, Tyrone almost broke my heart when I discovered that, while I was waiting at home for him each night, he was taking out my friends and cheating on me with them. But even then, I stayed with him, because I thought I loved him and because I didn't think anyone else would want me. When some of his friends tried to tell me how nasty he really was, and to convince me to get rid of him, I refused to listen. Like my mother, I thought I knew best, and I simply ignored any advice that might contradict my own opinions or interfere with what I wanted to do – even when it came from people who were supposed to be Tyrone's friends.

Tyrone and I had been together several months, and he was still waiting to go to court for the violent assault he'd committed before we met, when he came home one day with a proposition.

'The solicitor says I'd probably get a shorter sentence if you were pregnant with my child,' he told me, running his fingers along my arm in the way that always gave me goose bumps.

I was 16 and still at school, and although I'd never even considered having a baby, I'd probably have done anything Tyrone asked me to do. So I stopped taking the pill. But I still hadn't fallen pregnant by the time he went to trial and was sentenced to two years in jail.

His dad had laid out a very large sum of money for his bail, otherwise I don't think he'd have turned up at the court, because he knew that he'd be going to prison. The fact that I hadn't managed to become pregnant seemed to bother him less than it bothered me: I felt that I'd let him down, whereas he just shrugged his shoulders and said, 'Something else will turn up.'

I was devastated that he'd been taken away from me. I'd

finally found someone to love me and take care of me –
although in reality he didn't do either – and he'd been
sent to prison. It seemed so unfair – although the truth
was that, without any provocation, he'd viciously attacked
and seriously injured a young lad he just happened to
come across when he was drunk.

While Tyrone was in prison, we wrote to each other
every day and I never missed a visit. Every month, I'd
make the one-hour journey from my home with his
mother and sister, and Tyrone and I would talk about the
life we were going to live together when he got out. I
believed it all. I *needed* to be able to imagine myself in the
future, however unlikely were the plans I was making, and
I needed to believe that I wouldn't be all alone. Which is
why I suspended my common sense and allowed myself to
look forward to being 'happy ever after', determinedly
ignoring the fact that I was extremely unlikely to find
happiness with a vicious criminal who beat me up when
he was drunk and slept with my friends behind my back.

After a life lived with my mother – and years of being
abused by Carl – I had no expectations of anything better.
Although I hadn't forgotten the good life I'd lived with
my grandparents for a while, the memory of it only
served to highlight the contrast between my past and my
present and to make me feel that I was now living the life
I really deserved. I treasured the good memories and tried

to be realistic about not wishing for a future I was clearly never going to have.

While Tyrone was in prison, I left school and started working full time at the garden centre where I'd had a Saturday job. That was when I stopped using Carl's surname and reverted to my father's. I'd been too embarrassed to do it while I was at school, because it would have felt like drawing attention to myself and raising questions about my home life, which was something I wanted people to know as little about as possible. But it felt good to have broken that final connection with Carl and not to have to say his name any more.

A few months into his sentence, Tyrone came up for parole. It didn't seem likely it would be granted if the only place he had to go back to was the squat where he'd been living when we met. So my mother agreed that he could come and live at our house. But when the parole officer paid us a visit, it didn't take him long to realise that releasing even a hamster into the care of my mother would probably not have been a very good idea. I think it was something she said about my relationship with Tyrone that finally sealed his fate, though, and the parole officer put in a recommendation that his request for parole should be turned down. I was heartbroken, and furious with my mother for messing up Tyrone's chance of being released.

A few days later, the police turned up at our house and asked me if I'd seen him.

'I don't know what you mean,' I told the policeman. 'He's in prison.'

'When did you last hear from him?' the other policeman asked me.

I'd learned how to tell a convincing lie from a very good teacher – my mother. But this time I didn't have to lie, because I really didn't know what was going on.

The policemen watched me closely for a moment and I stared back at them defiantly.

'He escaped this morning,' one of them told me eventually.

Tyrone had been held in an open prison, and apparently he'd simply walked out, stolen a car and driven away.

I tried not to grin as I said, 'It's the first I've heard about it.'

'Well, you make sure you let us know if you hear anything else,' one of the policemen told me. 'You don't want to get yourself tied up with this lad, love. He's trouble. And he'll make trouble for you, too.'

I just laughed. What did some dreary, middle-aged policeman know about anything? Tyrone loved me and we were going to have a life together.

The policeman shrugged his shoulders. 'Harbouring

an escaped prisoner is a crime,' he warned me. 'So if he *does* get in touch with you and you don't let us know…'

I looked past him, towards the street, to show him I was no longer listening, and after a moment he shrugged again. Then they both walked back to the police car and drove away.

Half an hour later, I was in the living room when I heard the sound of something tapping against the window. I looked up and there was Tyrone, grinning at me. He pointed towards the side of the house and I rushed to open the back door. When I let him in, he held a finger to his lips and then hugged me so hard he almost squeezed all the air out of me. Unknown to me, he'd been hiding in the garden the whole time the police had been talking to me. I felt a rush of love for him: he must have known the police would pay me a visit, but he'd wanted to see me so badly he'd risked getting caught and had come anyway.

For several days after that, there was almost always a police car parked down the road from the house, and I began to get used to opening the front door and finding several policemen standing there with a search warrant, demanding to search my bedroom. They were looking for Tyrone's clothes in my wardrobe or for any other signs that might indicate he'd been there, and each time they came they warned me again that I was playing with fire and that Tyrone was far more dangerous than I understood. But I still refused to listen. I was in love and I felt wanted. And nothing else mattered.

Tyrone stayed in squats and with various members of his family and visited me whenever he could. He'd leave his car several streets away and walk down the alley to see if the police car was parked at the end of our road, before slipping down the side of the house and knocking on the back door. We'd keep my bedroom window open while he was in the house, so that he could jump out on to the garage roof and escape if he had to. Inevitably, though, with the police never far away, it became increasingly difficult for him to visit me, and I was torn between wanting to see him and being afraid he'd get caught. Eventually, we realised it was becoming too risky, and Tyrone decided to stay away for a while and do various jobs – all of them illegal – so that he could save up enough money for us to move away from the area together.

I was just 17, and although the thought of living with Tyrone was exciting, I knew it would also mean living on the run from the police. I constantly reviewed the pros and cons in my mind. Tyrone said he loved me, and when he wasn't drunk I was able to convince myself that that was true. I thought I loved him, too, and I was certain that if I didn't go with him, I'd never find anyone else who wanted me. And, after all, what was there to keep me at home? My mother was a hopeless alcoholic and not much of a mother by any standards. From the moment I was born, she'd done me more harm than good in countless ways. On the other hand, though, she *was* my mother – and, aside from Chris, pretty much all the family I had – and I knew she wouldn't survive on her own without me. I was surprised how anxious I felt at the thought of having to leave her and my dismal home.

I had no one to talk to or confide in, and as the days passed I became increasingly apprehensive and uncertain. Then, at almost the very last moment, I decided I couldn't go away with Tyrone. I knew I wouldn't be welcomed by his friends and family and, when it came to it, I simply couldn't bring myself to abandon my mother.

It was a relief to have made some sort of decision, although the thought of being alone made me panic – which is why I started seeing Keith.

Keith was a flashy drug dealer who was more than ten years older than me. He drove around the neighbourhood in an expensive car with the sort of tinted windows that draw attention to the fact that the driver has something to hide.

I hadn't seen Tyrone for some time, but when he found out I was seeing Keith, he came to my house. My mother answered the door, while I flattened myself against the wall of the upstairs landing and listened. Tyrone begged her to let him see me so that he could say goodbye. He promised he wouldn't lose his temper and hit me, and she allowed herself to be persuaded, as she always did, whatever anyone told her.

'Anna, it's Tyrone,' she called, without moving away from the door, which must have made it obvious to Tyrone that I'd been within earshot all the time.

I took a deep breath and walked slowly down the stairs and into the hallway. The sadness I could see in Tyrone's eyes seemed genuine as he asked me if it was true that I was seeing Keith.

'Yes, it's true,' I shouted at him. 'Well, what did you expect me to do? You never came round. Did you think I was just going to wait for you for ever?'

'But I thought you knew where I was,' he answered. 'We talked about it – me doing jobs so that we could get some money together and buy a trailer to live in. I told you I'd come back when I'd saved enough. I thought you'd wait for me.'

I felt terrible. Throughout all the years since I'd lived with my grandparents, no one had ever done what they'd promised me they'd do. Nothing in my life had ever been permanent, and certainly no one had ever gone to any trouble on my behalf. But I knew it was already too late. I was entangled with Keith, and he wasn't the sort of person who'd just stand by and let me walk away with someone else. And I still had the same fears I'd had for my mother when I made the decision not to go on the run with Tyrone.

Maybe what he was telling me was true. Maybe he had just been working hard to save money for our future. What was certain, though, was that if I really had had a chance to escape my miserable existence and have someone of my own, I'd blown it.

Tyrone also kept his promise to my mother and didn't hit me. He simply said goodbye and told me to look after myself, and then I watched him walk away, closed the front door and ran up the stairs to my room, where I lay on my bed and cried for everything I thought I'd lost.

15

The decision that changed my life

I REALISED AS soon as Tyrone had gone that I'd made a mistake. My relationship with my mother was volatile and dysfunctional and mainly involved fighting and screaming at each other. And I was completely intimidated by Keith, who was a vicious bully and a control freak. He'd tell me what to wear, which of my friends I could see and which of them I had to drop, and when he organised a birthday party for me, he refused to allow me to invite a single friend of my own. He was deliberately and systematically separating me from my own world and drawing me into his, so that I'd be completely under his thumb and dependent on him. He kept going on and on at me about moving in with him. But, fortunately, I had just enough common sense left – or perhaps just enough of an instinct for self-preservation – to refuse. Because I knew that, however grim and depressing it was to live at home with my mother, I'd never get away from Keith if I put myself in a position where he was able to control me 24 hours a day.

I hadn't had a period for a couple of months, since before I started seeing Keith, and it began to dawn on me that I might be pregnant. Just the thought of it made me panic, because the baby would be Tyrone's – an escaped prisoner who was on the run and who I'd probably never see again. I didn't have anyone to turn to for advice or even just to talk to about it, so I tried to push it to the back of my mind, telling myself that it wasn't something I needed to deal with anyway until I knew for certain that the problem existed.

The thought of having a baby filled me with almost paralysing anxiety. I was just 17, and I appeared to be repeating all the mistakes my mother had made. I was hurtling down a road towards self-destruction, just as she was doing, and, like her, I seemed to have no interest in looking for the brake pedal.

One day, when I turned up at Keith's house and let myself in with the key he'd insisted on giving me, I found him in bed with the girl who was my best friend at school. I knew Keith didn't really care about anyone except himself, and I should have realised that he wasn't the sort of man to be faithful to one person. But what shocked and hurt me most of all was finding him with my friend. She must have known how I felt, because she lay there, clutching the sheet under her chin with both hands and looking terrified.

I went crazy, grabbing everything within reach and hurling it at them both, screaming obscenities as I ran backwards and forwards between the door and the end of the bed. Eventually, when I couldn't find anything else to throw at them, I stormed out of the bedroom and ran down the stairs. I could hear Keith calling after me, 'Babe. Wait a minute, Babe. I can explain.' And as I slammed the front door, I almost wished I'd waited to hear his explanation of what it was they were actually doing, stark naked in bed together in the middle of the afternoon!

Even though I didn't love Keith, it still felt like a slap in the face. I kept on making wrong decisions, and so I kept on being disappointed. It was inevitable; I should have known that. Because of the choices I was making, disappointment was waiting for me around every corner. But, each time, I just hoped that somehow, this time, everything would turn out all right. It wasn't ever going to happen, and deep down I knew it, which is probably why I felt so stupid for believing it might – particularly with someone like Keith.

I went home that day and told my mother I thought I might be pregnant, and that, if I was, Tyrone was the father.

To my mother, there was no such thing as a secret – at least, not when it concerned anyone other than herself. She told everyone everything, including the most intimate and embarrassing details of anything related to Chris and me. So I knew it was foolish to tell her something so private. But I'd reached rock bottom and I had no one else to talk to. I just couldn't go on keeping everything bottled up inside me any longer, however sensible it would have been to do so. Just like I'd done when I got involved with Keith – and so many other times in my life – I told myself that this time it would be all right; this time my mother would be sympathetic and understanding and, rather than blabbing to anyone and everyone, she'd give me good advice and help me to deal with this latest crisis. Of course, she let me down, and it wasn't long before word spread that I was pregnant.

A few days after I'd spoken to my mother, I was walking along the road near our house when a car pulled up beside me. I looked down and saw one of Tyrone's brothers leering up at me from the driver's seat.

He wound down his window, stared pointedly at my stomach for a moment and then said, 'Someone told me you're pregnant.'

He was with three of his mates, and I began to feel uneasy, although I managed to sound more bored than anxious as I replied, 'Yeah, so? Have you come to congratulate me?'

This time, he looked directly into my face when he spoke, and I felt the hairs on the back of my neck stand up. 'Someone told me that Tyrone's the baby's father.'

I looked away and he gave a short, unpleasant laugh.

'I told them they'd got that bit wrong. Because Tyrone's got a new girlfriend – a girl his family likes…this time. And we'd be really, really upset if you tried to get back into his life.'

He reached out and touched my arm. It was a gesture that might have appeared to a casual onlooker to be friendly, but it was actually a clear indication to me that he was in control as he said, 'So, tell me, *is* Tyrone the baby's father?'

I wanted to snatch my arm away and tell him to fuck off. But instead I looked down at my feet and answered, 'No.'

He patted my arm a couple of times and then withdrew his hand and asked, 'So, who *is* the father?'

He spoke slowly, as though talking to an idiot, and I had to resist the urge to reach through the open window of the car and punch his stupid, smug, bully's face as I said, 'I don't know. It's not Tyrone though.'

'So there's no reason for Tyrone to know anything about it?' It was clearly a statement, although he made it sound like a question.

He revved the engine of his car, filling the air with noise and oily fumes, so that he almost had to shout,

'After all, you've got the health of your baby to think about now, as well as your own.' Then he pulled away from the kerb and sped off down the street.

I'd already told my mother that the baby would definitely be Tyrone's, but she refused to accept that it wasn't Keith's. I think she was afraid I might leave her and go off with Tyrone, and although she treated me like shit, she knew she couldn't manage without me. Keith was almost 30 and everyone who knew him had heard him say how much he wanted to have a son of his own. And, as usual, my mother was thinking about herself rather than about what might be best for me when she decided to take matters into her own hands and tell him that the baby was his.

I was furious with her when I found out what she'd done. But she never apologised for anything she ever did, and this time was no exception.

'You should thank me,' she told me huffily. 'I've done you a favour. Tyrone's gone, but Keith's still here.' Then she wiped an imaginary tear from her eye and added dramatically, 'I want my grandchild to have a dad.'

I had a sudden urge to slap her. Calling my unborn child *her grandchild* was typical of her need to make everything all about her. And it was news to me that she considered being the child of an absent father to be a handicap, as she'd never once shown any understanding to my brother and me while we were growing up without *our* father. I saw through her, though, and I knew that all she really cared about was making sure I stayed and didn't abandon her. And, in her mind, that meant that Keith had to be the father of my child, or at least he had to think he was.

I hadn't seen Keith since the day I'd caught him in bed with my friend, but when I saw him at a nightclub shortly after I'd had the conversation with my mother, it was clear he was convinced that the baby was his. Like my mother, he was someone who could easily persuade himself to believe that whatever he wanted to be true *was* true. So I asked him if he'd have a paternity test when the baby was born, and he agreed.

I didn't see him again after that until I was nearing the end of my pregnancy, when we bumped into each other at a party and he told me, 'I've always wanted a son, and I don't care who the mother is.'

I WAS TOTALLY alone throughout my pregnancy, and by the time Christmas came round, I was looking forward to spending the day with my mother and my brother and to being able to pretend we were just like any other, real, family.

Christmas morning started off well, and we were about to start preparing our Christmas dinner when my mother told us she was popping out to see a friend who lived nearby, 'Just to wish her a Merry Christmas.' Two hours later, she fell in through the front door of our house and lay on the floor in the hallway, laughing and mumbling to herself, totally drunk. As I looked down at her, I could feel my eyes filling up with hot tears of frustration and disappointment. I brushed them away angrily with the back of my hand and as my mother staggered to her feet she hissed at me, 'It's fucking Christmas, for Christ's sake.' Then she opened the door of the living room, lay down on the floor and passed out.

I was still standing in the hallway, trying to decide what to do, when Chris pushed past me, opened the front door and, without looking at me, said, 'I'm going to Joe's. I'll have my meal there.'

I walked into the kitchen, stood by the sink and stared out into the back garden, wondering angrily why I'd ever thought the day would turn out differently. My mother always let me down; she couldn't really help it. So why had I allowed myself to believe that this time would be any different?

I was five months pregnant and completely alone. I put a hand on my swelling stomach and felt a familiar wave of panic wash over me. How was I going to manage when my baby was born? What was I doing even thinking of bringing into the world a child that was going to be dependent on *me* – someone who couldn't make a good decision to save her life?

I didn't normally wallow in self-pity, but I began to cry as I thought of all the other pregnant women in the country who were spending Christmas Day with their partners and families. Why couldn't I be one of them? Why did I only ever get tied up with losers and criminals? Why was my life such a mess?

I walked slowly up the stairs to my bedroom, sat on my bed and tried to count my blessings and think about all the people in the world who were far worse off than I was. Suddenly, an image of Carl came into my head. I could almost smell the stench of stale tobacco and alcohol that was always on his breath, and I could see clearly the nasty, leering expression he used to have on his face when he came into my bedroom at night. I hadn't thought about him at all in months. Wondering why I'd done so now, I lay down on my bed and began to sob silently into my pillow.

In the evening, after spending the day alone in my bedroom, I checked on my mother, covered her with a blanket where she lay, dead to the world, on the living-room floor, and then went to my friend's house. And that's where I was when my mother turned up a couple of hours later, still drunk.

'I'd been drinking shots,' she told me, laughing like a

naughty child about what had happened earlier in the day. Then her tone became wheedling as she added, 'I'm okay now, though, and I don't want to be all alone on Christmas Day. Come home, Anna. I need someone to keep me company. Pleeeeease.'

It was as though someone had flicked a switch and turned my brain off, and as I lunged at my mother and started punching her, all I could think was how hurt and resentful I felt.

'You selfish fucking bitch!' I screamed at her. 'What about us? You promised we were going to have a day together, like a normal family. But you don't care about us enough to be able to keep off the booze for even just a few hours.'

I'd rarely hit my mother, even on the many occasions when she'd attacked me without warning. This time, though, I completely lost it, and my friend and her father had to intervene and pull us off each other.

AS MY PREGNANCY progressed, I became increasingly frightened by the prospect of having to look after a baby on my own. What seemed even more terrifying, though, was imagining that baby growing into a child and going to school, and it was that thought that led to my becoming obsessed by the idea that I couldn't bring a child up on the estate we lived on. We'd been on the housing list for ten years, but it doesn't help your chances of being rehoused if your current neighbours are constantly making complaints about you because of all the trouble you cause, and if the police are regularly called to your house to break up fights, or worse. Even in the rough neighbourhood we lived in, we stood out as being the neighbours from hell. So I realised that the council was hardly likely to move us to somewhere we'd be even more of a socially unacceptable nuisance.

In the early spring, I went into labour and was admitted to hospital. During the birth, my son became distressed while he was still in the womb and he stopped breathing. For weeks I'd felt scared and alone, and in many ways I'd been dreading the thought of becoming a mother. But, suddenly, when there seemed to be a very real possibility that my son wouldn't live to see the light of day, I desperately wanted him to survive.

As the delivery room began to fill with doctors, I tried to follow their instructions to 'Breathe, breathe', and then to 'Push, keep pushing'. And eventually my son was born.

Immediately, the doctors rushed him to the other side of the room. They all seemed to be talking at the same time, their voices blocking out the sound of my son's first cry. And then I realised that he wasn't crying; he wasn't making any sound at all. I think I shouted out, although it may just have been in my head, but I definitely reached out my hand and clutched at the wrist of one of the nurses as I asked her, the panic clear in my voice, 'Is he breathing? Is he alive?'

'The doctors are giving him an injection to try to make him breathe.' The nurse patted my arm and I was frightened by the sympathy and sadness I could see in her eyes.

Tears trickled down the side of my face and mingled with the sweat that had already dampened the pillow under my head. And, just like my grandmother had done all those years ago, I began to whisper, 'Please God. Please God. Please God.'

This time, though, it seemed that God was listening, because after a few seconds I heard a tiny, feeble sound like a kitten mewling. Then someone held my son in front of me just long enough for me to touch his blue, wrinkled little face before they put him in an incubator and wheeled him quickly from the room.

Later, when I'd been taken to the hospital ward, they brought the incubator and placed it beside my bed, and I lay on my side looking at my beautiful son and remembering, from the days when I lived with my grandparents, what it felt like to really love someone. Ironically, though, it was my mother who had to show me how to pick my baby up and cuddle him. I'd spent so many years of my life perfecting the art of hiding my feelings that I even felt embarrassed to hold my own son.

I looked around me at all the other women in all the other beds on the ward, and at all their husbands and partners, and I wondered what the hell I was supposed to do now. I had, literally, nothing to give my son except a second-hand Moses basket, and I was afraid that, emotionally at least, I might need him far more than he needed me.

A COUPLE OF days after I took my baby home from the hospital, Keith came to see him.

'He looks just like me,' he told me, looking into the Moses basket and touching the tiny hand. 'I don't need a paternity test to know I'm his father.'

The next day, I was in the living room when there was a knock on the front door and, a few seconds later, Tyrone walked in.

'I've come to see my son,' he said, tossing a wad of money on to the sofa.

'I've told Keith he's his,' I answered, standing beside Tyrone as he looked down at the peacefully sleeping baby.

Without a word, he scooped up the wad of notes and walked out, leaving his son in the care of a penniless, clueless teenager and her alcoholic mother.

When my aunts came to see the baby, it was clear that they were disgusted with me. One of them told me that my grandmother would be turning in her grave if she knew what was going on, and another wanted to take my son and bring him up herself, so that he'd have a better life than the one he was clearly going to have with me. I could see the sense in what she was saying, but I told her I'd be able to manage, because my mother had promised to help me.

'Your mother couldn't even be bothered to look after her *own* children,' she sneered. 'What makes you think she's going to bother looking after someone else's?'

It was a fair question, and I couldn't blame my aunt for thinking I wouldn't be a good mother. It seemed to be an opinion shared by everyone who knew me – and, in fact, one that I held myself. I had no money, no parents who were realistically going to be able to help and guide me, and nothing to give my baby, not even a cot or a pram to put him in.

A few days later, I 'borrowed' a stolen credit card from one of our lodgers while he was out and bought my son a cot, bedding and all the other bits and pieces I couldn't afford. Then I slipped the credit card back where I'd found it amongst the lodger's belongings.

It was the norm where we lived to see people arriving home late at night with things they'd burgled, or with tyres they'd stolen from cars, which they'd left standing on bricks, and stealing credit cards wasn't really even considered a crime, because lots of people did it. For example, I went into a shoe shop in town one day and came face to face with a family I knew, who lived near us on the estate. The mum was standing at the till, and when I said 'Hello', she just nodded curtly and then turned her back on me. I was a bit surprised, but I turned away too and I'd started looking at the shoes when the dad wandered over, stood beside me and whispered not to mention their surname, because his wife was buying shoes for the whole family with a stolen credit card.

As children grow up, they accept and absorb the morality of the adults who have the greatest influence on them – normally their parents – and most of the people on that estate had a completely distorted understanding of what was right and acceptable. I can remember a boy a bit younger than me boasting to me one Christmas that he and his mates had robbed a family of all their Christmas presents except the kid's bike. He almost puffed out his chest with pride at the thought of his superior sensitivity, and I wasn't even shocked, because it was just the way of life.

After my son was born, however, I became even more obsessed by the thought of moving to a better neighbourhood. We'd made numerous applications to the council asking to be moved, but each time an inspector had come to the house and given us a list of the things we'd have to do before they'd even consider our request.

The list included totally refurbishing the house and garden – which, the inspector told us, looked like the back end of the Somme – and, realistically, there was almost nothing on it that was going to get done. So we kept getting knocked back, until it became clear that they had no intention of rehousing us at all.

I knew that there was an empty council house on a much nicer estate not far away from where we were living, and one day I asked if we could have the key, just to have a look. When my mother and I arrived, I opened the front door, walked into the empty living room and almost cried. The house was everything I wanted. It had clean, airy rooms without a trace of mildew or any water running down the walls, and it was in a nice area where you wouldn't be ashamed to live and bring up a child. I knew that if only we could move to somewhere like that and start again, I could keep it clean and make it into a real home for my son.

As I stood there, looking out of the living-room window at the little back garden, I felt a rush of resolve, and suddenly I knew what I had to do. I was determined that my child wasn't going to live in our house; he was going to have a home just like this. In fact, he was going to have *this* home.

Later that day, we returned to the empty house with our tatty bits of furniture and moved in.

When the council realised what we'd done, a council officer came to see us. We pretended we'd misunderstood and that we thought we'd been given permission, and, at last, my mother's ability to lie convincingly was put to good use.

'But they gave us the key,' she told the irritated council officer, with an expression on her face of such credible innocence that I had to turn away to hide my smile. 'They said we could come and see if we liked it. And we did. They wouldn't have told us to do that if we couldn't have it, would they?' She laughed at the very thought of such a ridiculous idea.

'You knew perfectly well that you were not being given permission to move into this house,' the man snapped at my mother. 'You're going to have to pack up your stuff' – he looked round the room at our shabby, broken furniture with an expression of thinly veiled disgust – 'and go back from whence you came.'

There were a few people on the estate who already knew us, and a few more who knew our reputation, and when they heard we'd moved in, they got up a petition to try to have us evicted. They claimed, reasonably enough, that we'd have parties and fights and there'd be criminals and troublemakers at the house. In the end, though, the council let us stay, probably because no one there could face the idea of the battle that lay ahead if they tried to get us out.

The new estate was completely different from where we used to live. Quite a few people had bought their council houses, and all the houses and gardens were nice and well maintained. What struck me particularly, though, was that people didn't know everyone else's business; they just went to work – a novelty in itself after living on an estate where only the minority of adults had jobs – and then they came home and got on with their own lives.

But ultimately the residents' petition proved unnecessary, as, once we'd moved in, my mother's parties stopped. She'd always been afraid of being left on her own, and often when she was drunk, she'd cry and threaten to kill herself if I left her – and she knew I wouldn't live in the new house with my son if the parties continued. Another reason they stopped was because we'd been careful not to let my mother's friends know where we were going. Some of them tried to track us down, though, and one night a group of them turned up at the house of a friend of mine, asking where we were, and then beat up her father when he lied and said they didn't know.

The club was still within walking distance and my mum still drank there, or got the bus into town and went to a pub, and she'd still occasionally bring a man home with her. But it was nothing compared to what she used to be like.

Not long after we'd moved into our new home, I met Ken – another recently released prisoner whose idea of 'taking me out' was to turn up at the house after the pubs had closed. I was 19 when I fell pregnant with his child. As soon as I told him, he left me and started seeing someone else. And by the time I was four months pregnant, I was seeing Dee.

16

Bereaved, betrayed and determined

DEE DIDN'T WANT to be lumbered with another man's child and he told me he'd only stay with me if I had an abortion. I was already struggling to support my son and I couldn't see any alternative, although it was a really difficult decision to make. I loved my son, and it felt as though I'd be killing another baby who would have been just like him. I cried a lot, both before and after I'd had the abortion, and then, two weeks later, I went to Dee's house and found him in bed with another girl.

It felt like the worst betrayal of all. I was racked with guilt about what I'd done, and also, without really realising it, I'd been mourning the loss of my unborn child. All the feelings I'd been suppressing came out in a rush of furious anger as I hurled myself across the room and attacked them both. I kept hitting and punching them as hard as I could, and the girl just lay there, trying to protect her face with her arms. I was shocked and hurt, but most of all I was hysterical with grief at the thought that I'd had an abortion mainly because Dee had promised to stay with me if I did.

Later that day, the police arrived at my house and I was arrested and charged with ABH and criminal damage. When I went to court for the trial, the girl didn't turn up to give evidence against me, but I was found guilty of ABH, fined and given 12 months' conditional discharge.

Fortunately, being arrested wasn't seen as anything unusual or shocking by the people I mixed with. And nor was being the mother of a young child and still going out and getting drunk every weekend. I wasn't consciously aware of it at the time, but I was searching for someone to love me, although unfortunately, mostly because of what Carl had done to me, I had a very confused idea about what love was, and I don't think I'd have recognised it even if I'd found it. In any case, I had such low self-esteem that I didn't believe someone like me deserved to be treated any better than I was treated by the low-lifes I came into contact with. So I continued to allow myself to be used and abused by anyone who showed even the slightest interest in me.

Then, one day, when I was changing my son's nappy, I looked down at him as he lay smiling and gurgling and waving his arms in the jerky, excited way he always did, and I thought, *What the hell am I doing?* It was like a physical shock, as if someone had punched me in the stomach, and I had to grasp the edge of the table to steady myself as the answer to the question came to me: *I'm giving my son the same miserable, dysfunctional life my mother gave me. A life I hated.*

I thought about all the times my mother had failed to be there for me; all the times she'd been too drunk to listen when I had something important I wanted to tell her; and all the times she'd let me down because she'd rather drink with strangers and people who didn't care about her than spend time with her own children. That was exactly what I was doing to *my* child, and that was exactly the sort of mother I was going to become. I could envisage the miserable, dead-end life my son was going to live because he had a mother who would be lying in a drunken stupor whenever he needed her most. And I knew how he was going to feel as he got older, because I'd felt that way myself for as long as I could remember.

That was the day I stopped drinking – and I've never touched a drop of alcohol since.

When I was 21, I started seeing Ken again – the father of my aborted child – and it wasn't long before he'd moved in to live with me at my mother's house. Although he spent every weekend at the pub, and was often arrested for fighting when he was drunk, he was good to my son, who idolised him. A year later, I gave birth to Ken's daughter, and it finally seemed as though I'd become part of the one thing I'd always longed for: a family.

Our daughter was 18 months old when I decided I'd had enough of living off the social, and I started to work full-time in a factory. When I was growing up, by the time my mother had put aside the money to buy her week's supply of alcohol, there was often not enough left to buy food, and I was determined my children weren't going to live like that. They were going to live in a nice, clean house with decent furniture, and they were going to eat good food every single day of the week.

My mother agreed to look after the children while I was working. I know that sounds as though I must have lost my mind, but although she was a terrible mother, she turned out to be a really wonderful grandmother. One day, when my son was just three years old, he'd found her in bed unconscious and covered in vomit after she'd tried to commit suicide. She'd had to be rushed to hospital to have her stomach pumped, and afterwards she'd been devastated by the fact that it had been her grandson who'd found her in such a terrible state. And because she loved my children and she knew I wouldn't let her look after them unless she was totally sober, she'd started to restrict her drinking to the weekends. For the first time in her life, it seemed that something mattered enough for her to make the effort to get her act together for at least a few hours every day.

Ken opened a bar with a friend, which quickly became popular and began to bring in a lot of money. So, after just four years of monotonous work in a factory, I was able to leave and go to night school to learn the skills I needed to get a better-paid job in an office. I worked hard, and although I didn't really need to work for financial reasons, it gave me a sense of purpose and made me feel as though I was living the normal life I'd always wanted to live, and it wasn't long before I was promoted.

I think that, like many people who've experienced an abusive childhood, I had to work harder than anyone else at everything I did, because I had to try to prove to everyone that I wasn't useless and worthless, as I'd always been told I was. Mostly, though, I was trying to prove it to myself, and that's something few of us ever really manage to do. Something else many abuse survivors share is the drive to create order in our lives, because we always feel that if we relax for even a moment, the chaos we lived with as children will come rushing in like a tidal wave and overwhelm us again.

I felt, too, that people were looking down on me. I'd be talking to someone in the office, and they'd be listening to whatever it was I was saying, when I'd suddenly become convinced that although they seemed to be taking me seriously, they were actually laughing at me, because they knew who I really was and where I'd come from. I'd break out in a cold sweat and lose track of what I was saying, and sometimes I'd have to stop in the middle of a sentence so that I could escape. In reality, though, I don't suppose anyone had any suspicion that I wasn't the respectable mother, partner and work colleague I appeared to be.

Constantly looking over my shoulder and being afraid of the shadow cast by my childhood also meant that, as well as working really hard at my job, I made sure that my children were always immaculate – clean and shining from head to toe; that my garden was the neatest and best tended of any in the neighbourhood and that my house was, quite literally, clean enough for you to eat your meals off the floor.

When my son was five years old, he made a new friend, a little boy called Mickey, who everyone else hated. Mickey was one of half a dozen children born to the same mother, but all with different fathers. His current stepdad treated him badly, and his mother simply didn't care about him. The first time I met him, he turned up on our doorstep on a very cold day in the winter wearing a jumper that was full of holes and with his feet poking out of the ends of his shoes. I asked him where he lived, and whether his mother would be worried about him, and he looked surprised as he assured me she wouldn't. It turned out that he'd walked a long way trying to find our house, because he wanted to see my son, who was the only friend he had. He stayed with us for a while and then I took him home in the car, and by chance shortly afterwards, his family was rehoused temporarily just across the road from us.

No normal person likes to see children being mistreated, either mentally or physically, and as the house where Mickey lived gradually became more run-down and filthy while his mother watched TV all day and the children roamed the streets and got into mischief, I knew exactly how that little boy must be feeling. He began to spend more and more time at our house. He'd eat with us almost every night, and we'd take him with us whenever we went swimming or out for a meal – he'd never eaten in a restaurant before. On one occasion, he stayed with us for two weeks without ever going home, and his mother never once came looking for him. One day, I discovered that he'd been banned from the school bus for fighting and that for the last few days his mother had simply left him to walk the three miles to school and back. So I started driving him there in the mornings and then picking him up in the afternoons.

It felt as though I had to do for Mickey all the things I wished someone had done for me when I was a child.

And then eventually the family moved away and the two boys lost contact with each other. Later, I heard Mickey had got into trouble with the police and gone to prison, and I was sad that I hadn't been able to do something to help him. It was the road I'd always thought I was going to travel myself, but maybe I'd avoided it because of the seeds my grandparents had sown – in my mind and in my heart – when I'd lived with them for two years as a little girl.

Whatever the reason I was saved from the future that seemed to have been mapped out for me, I know that when children start getting into trouble, you need to look at their family relationships. If there's no one in their lives who loves them and cares enough about them to teach them right from wrong, and there's no one to teach them to have self-respect, then how can you expect them to respect anyone else?

When my children were young, I rarely saw my father. He spent quite a lot of time with my brother Chris and his wife, but he wasn't interested in me or my children, although I never gave up hope that one day things might be different.

He'd always been a heavy smoker and drinker, and he had a family history of heart disease, and one morning when he was in his mid-forties, he got up to go to work as usual, had a heart attack and died.

His death hit me harder than I could ever have imagined. Not because I'd lost someone I loved, but because I'd lost the chance of ever having a good relationship with my dad. For years, I'd clung to the hope that one day he'd be proud of me. And now that hope was gone and I felt cheated. It had been ten years since I'd tracked him down, just before my grandmother died, and since then I'd only seen him a handful of times. It hurt me that my brother had never confronted him and asked him why he treated me the way he did. But, after my father died, Chris told me that he had wanted to get to know me. I'd like to think that was true, even though it was too late anyway.

When I was 16 and I found my father, I assumed he'd love me automatically, simply because he was my dad, and that I'd love him too. In reality, though, we were strangers, with nothing but bad memories of the past we'd briefly shared. It was a realisation I found hard to deal with at the time. I'd been so certain that when we met again, everything would be great between us; that we'd be like any normal father and daughter. But that hadn't happened. We didn't love each other; in fact, we didn't even like each other. After that meeting, I'd sent him a Father's Day card, but he hadn't acknowledged it, and I think it was then that I realised I couldn't stand the sight of him or even bear the sound of his voice. When my two eldest children were born, he'd wanted nothing to do with them either, claiming that he was unhappy about becoming a grandfather so young.

After he died, one of my aunts dug out an old family photo album and I saw a photo of my father on the day he married my mother. It was the first time I'd seen a picture of him as a young man, and I was struck by how similar he looked to the first boy I ever willingly slept with. They were almost the spitting image of each other – the same build, the same closely cropped hairstyle, and the same big eyes and long eyelashes. I'd always told myself I didn't want or need my father's love. But as I looked at that photograph, I wondered if I'd been searching all my life for someone to take his place and love me.

Going to my father's funeral seemed to be the right thing to do, and I suppose it was also something I needed to do for my own sake. His mother had developed dementia by that time and I was sad that she couldn't recognise or remember me, her eldest granddaughter. The rest of his family chose to ignore me. They must have wondered why I was crying about the death of a father who hadn't cared about me and who I rarely saw. But I think what I was really upset about was that, having lived my entire life in the hope that better things were just around the corner, it was hard to come to terms with the fact that now I'd never hear my father say he loved me and that he was sorry for the way he'd treated me. In reality, though, that was something that probably would never have happened, even if he'd lived to be a hundred.

I continued to work hard at my job, and I earned a decent salary, although Ken's business was going from strength to strength and we didn't really need the money. My third child was born when I was 30 and my fourth a year later, after which I didn't go back to work. We bought our house from the council and my mother moved into a flat nearby, which is where she was living when she met Dave. Unlike almost all the other boyfriends she'd ever had, Dave was a nice man, with a job and a house in Spain, where he often took her for holidays, and after a while they got married.

Things were going better for us all than I could ever have imagined.

I never tried to talk to my mother about my childhood or about the damage her behaviour had done to me in so many ways. But, despite all the things that had to remain unsaid between us, we'd developed a surprisingly good, if careful, relationship, which was based largely on our shared love for my children. Things were going so well with Ken's business that he'd opened another bar and we were eventually able to sell our little ex-council house and buy a large, airy, detached house not far away.

I should have been happy. But I seemed to have lost the

capacity for happiness. Although I loved my children with all my heart, and I was pleased that they were getting all the things I didn't have as a child – the material things as well as the love I'd always longed for – I still seemed unable ever to relax. I always felt as though there was more I could be doing for them, and I was always haunted by the fear that people would realise I wasn't really the person I was pretending to be.

I tried to remind myself that what had happened to me in my childhood wasn't my fault, but when Carl abused me he planted a tiny, destructive worm in my heart, which kept gnawing away at my self-respect and confidence. The best I could hope for was to be able to keep my depression locked up inside me so that I could get through each day and be ready to face the next one.

It sounds melodramatic to say that my children saved my life – and that they continue to do so every single day. But it's true, because without the thought of how terrible it would be for them, there were – and still are – many, many days on which I'd have given up the endless, exhausting battle to keep going and taken my own life.

WE'D BEEN IN our new house for a couple of years when I began to notice that Ken often let his phone ring without answering it. There'd already been the occasional sign that we might be running short of money, and then, one day, he told me he'd taken out a very large loan because he was having problems with the business.

'But I don't understand,' I told him. 'What's happened? Have people stopped coming to the bars? How can they be popular and making good money one minute, and then running at a loss the next?'

I thought he was going to hit me, but he just snarled, 'Don't interfere in things you don't understand,' and left the room.

A few days later, after the children had gone to bed and I was tidying the kitchen, he came in and sat down at the table.

'I'm going to have to remortgage the house,' he told me, and although his voice sounded casual, he refused to look me in the face.

'What do you mean? Why?' I asked, not really understanding what he was saying.

'Oh, it's nothing important.' I could tell he was starting to get irritated, and that he was struggling not to show it. 'I'll pay it back before the end of the year. I just need some money upfront to keep the business going.'

The thought of losing the house made me feel physically sick. To me, it wasn't just bricks and mortar; it represented respectability and acceptance for my children. It was a house in the sort of neighbourhood I'd always wanted to live in, a neighbourhood where normal people lived, with children who were contented and well cared for and who were going to have the opportunity to make something of their lives. I'd worked hard to drag myself up out of the filthy chaos of my childhood to live in that house, and I wasn't sure that the ragged remains of my self-esteem would survive losing it, because that would mean I'd failed, and I'd sworn to myself long ago that I wasn't, ever, going to let my children down.

'I just need you to sign the papers.' Ken was still refusing to look directly at me, and he was finding it increasingly difficult to hide his impatience.

'No!' I almost shouted. 'I'm not signing any papers. You can remortgage your share of the house, but you're not touching mine. This is all I've got, and I'm not going to risk losing it, not even to save the business. There *must* be another way.'

'There's no other way, you stupid bitch,' Ken screamed at me. 'Do you think I'd be doing it if there was another way? This is the *only* way. So just sign the fucking papers.'

I held out against him for as long as I could, while he shouted and threatened and swore at me. Then I signed the papers and went to bed, where I cried myself to sleep.

I hadn't had any idea about how bad things were with the business. It had all happened so quickly. I knew that Ken's business partner, Barry, had disappeared. But both bars had remained open after he'd gone and had, apparently, continued to be as popular as they'd ever been. And then debts had started to build up that Ken had refused to explain to me – not that he'd ever really discussed his business with me anyway.

Even after I'd signed away our security by enabling Ken to remortgage the house, he seemed to continue to become paler, older-looking and more strained with each day that passed. Eventually, when it seemed that he was near breaking point, he sat me down in the living room and explained what had really happened.

'After Barry left, these guys came to the bar,' he told me. 'They said Barry owed them money. They were debts that weren't connected with the bars, or with me, but they didn't care who paid them.'

His hands were trembling and as he leaned forward to pick up his glass, he splashed drink on to the sofa.

'It was a great deal of money,' he continued. 'More than a hundred K. I told them I didn't have that sort of cash, but they just said I had three days to find it. At first, they told me it was just one payment and that, once I'd paid it, they wouldn't need to bother me any more. I kept trying to get in touch with Barry, but he seemed to have disappeared off the face of the fucking earth. So I had no choice.'

After that, they kept coming back for more money, until Ken eventually told them that all his sources had run dry – which is when they'd held a gun to his head. He cried when he told me that, and when he said he'd thought he was going to die, all alone in the stockroom at the bar. He'd already borrowed from the bank and from every loan company he could think of, and then he'd remortgaged the house. In the end, he'd paid them more than half a million pounds.

'Why didn't you go to the police?' I asked, torn between sympathy for him and fury at the thought that we had nothing left, except huge debts we couldn't possibly ever pay back.

'I thought I could handle it,' he said, an edge of arrogant irritation creeping back into his voice. 'The first time, I believed them when they said it was just one payment. I thought Barry had left owing them some money and they'd just take it and go. But they kept coming back. Then they started threatening to wreck the bars and they told me they'd kill you and the kids if I didn't keep paying. So what else could I do?'

I wanted to scream at him, 'I hate you! I hate you!' I knew it wasn't fair to blame him – he'd been frightened and out of his depth and it had been far too late to back out by the time he realised they were never going to leave him alone. But I couldn't help it: everything we'd built up was starting to fall apart. We'd remortgaged the house for almost the full market value, and now we were going to have to sell it to pay off just one of the loans. We'd never get out of debt, however hard we worked.

The next day, we put the house up for sale. But before the agent had a chance to show anyone round, we decided to do a flit and go to Spain, where my mother was living with her new husband. We couldn't tell anyone what we were planning to do, and I felt like a child again, having to keep secrets. Within a few days, we'd packed up the house, taken the kids out of school and fled the country.

My eldest son has always been very close to my mother, but, of all the children, he was the one who found it most difficult to settle in Spain. The others were younger, and although they were initially upset about leaving behind everything and everyone they were used to, they soon adapted to their new life. But it was different for my eldest son: he was a teenager, with friends and a life of his own in England, and he started to become withdrawn and depressed. I worried about him constantly, and about how Ken and I were going to start our lives all over again.

I felt as though I'd suffered a bereavement. We'd lost everything and we were completely broke. It seemed so unfair, and I began to hate Ken. The house in England was empty and when the agent did eventually find a buyer for it, the price he offered was less than we owed on the mortgage. I deeply regretted having signed the papers to remortgage it, which I never would have done if Ken hadn't threatened and bullied me. I tried to tell myself that it was just a house; that what really mattered was that Ken and the children were safe and we were all together. But it was more than just a house to me. It was a symbol of all the things I didn't have when I was growing up, all the things I'd wanted my children to have, and all the things I'd worked so hard and overcome so much to get for them.

Whatever people like to think, everyone makes judgements based on appearances and first impressions – and not always without good reason. If you live in the dirtiest, most run-down house on the worst council estate in the area, people make assumptions about you, even when you're a child. They never stop to think that maybe you hate living there, that maybe you spend hours trying to combat the filth and make some sort of order out of the chaos, and maybe you'd give anything in the world to live somewhere nice with someone who cared about you. Because the truth is that no kids like 'living in their own shit', as our neighbours believed all those years ago.

I don't know how much Ken really cared about me. In the days before things started to go wrong, he *had* worked hard, but then he'd spent most of his non-working hours drinking with his mates, which meant that the only time he really gave me any attention was when he was drunk and spoiling for a fight. That hadn't mattered, though, because I'd never expected anyone to love me and because he'd provided for me and the children, which was the most I'd ever hoped for.

We'd been in Spain for three months when I suddenly felt as though I'd woken up. It was wrong that the children and I had lost our home. I hadn't signed the papers willingly; I'd had no choice at the time, because Ken had threatened me and told me that the people he'd got tied up with were going to kill him if he didn't raise the money to pay them off. I became obsessed with the belief that if there isn't a law to protect people in that sort of situation, then there should be. Our creditors hadn't needed to fight, because I'd just given in and let them take our home away from us.

My whole reason for staying alive is because I know my children need me. The nearest I come to feeling happy is when I know that they're happy. And as my eldest son became increasingly depressed, I felt as though I'd let him down. I'd spent my entire life trying to run away from something, and suddenly I realised that I could never escape the thing I was really running away from: me.

I didn't know what I was going to do, but I knew that I wasn't going to give up without a fight.

17
Fighting back

THE NEXT DAY, I told Ken and my mother and stepfather I was leaving. Then I packed suitcases for myself and the children, and two days later we were back in England, staying at my aunt's house. Ken followed us after a few days, but our relationship wasn't strong enough to survive so much stress, and we split up. The children and I moved back into the house, Ken rented a flat not far away, and I began to try to work out how I could fight the mortgage company for the right to continue to pay the mortgage on our home.

I knew it was going to be an uneven fight and I don't think I really held out much hope of winning against a large company and its team of legal experts. But it felt as though all my life people had been making me do things that clearly weren't fair or just, and I'd never even realised I might have the right to say, 'No. This isn't what I want.' On the occasions when I had tried to express an opinion, no one had listened to me; in fact, no one had ever seemed to hear me at all. So although I didn't know what I was going to do, I did know that I had to try to do *something*, because I was sick to death of being pushed around.

The mortgage company was in the process of taking us to court so that they could repossess our house, and Ken had given up. He'd been arrogant to think he could deal alone with the low-lifes he'd inadvertently become entangled with. He'd given them everything we had, as well as all the money he could borrow, before realising he might never be able to get them off his back. I knew he'd been really frightened when they'd threatened his life, so, in some ways, I could understand why he wanted to walk away from the whole mess, let the mortgage company have the house, and just be thankful he was still alive.

I was glad he hadn't been hurt, of course, but I was still furious with him for not going to the police right at the start. When I tried to explain to him what the house meant to me, he was defensive, shrugging his shoulders and saying spitefully, 'I can't see what you're moaning about. You came from a council estate. So, if we lose the house, you'll just be going back where you came from.'

And, although he was sneering at me, he'd actually identified what lay at the very heart of what losing the house meant to me. It wasn't the house as a material possession that mattered; it was what it represented. For as long as I can remember, ever since I was a small child and, first, my father ignored and disliked me, then Carl abused me, I've lived with the knowledge that I'm worthless – literally, worth nothing. There have been many, many days when, if it hadn't been for my children and for my own, immensely painful, childhood memories of finding my mother unconscious after she'd tried to commit suicide, I'd have killed myself without a second thought. But, however tempted I've been, I've never done it, because I know that, just like I needed my mother and suffered because she was never there for me, my children need me. The nice, clean, comfortable house I'd worked so hard for represented all the things I wanted to give them, including stability, a decent, well-ordered family life in a home they weren't ashamed to bring their friends to, and normality.

It wasn't living on a council estate that I objected to. It was all the terrible things in my childhood that would have been associated with taking that step backwards. It was as though my past was an animal with sharp teeth that was always snapping at my heels, waiting for me to stumble so that it could pounce and drag me back down into the nightmare from which I'd finally managed to escape. It was an image that haunted my dreams – both waking and asleep – and I knew it was my responsibility to prevent my children ever having to experience a childhood like the one I'd had. I'd worked hard to build a protective cocoon around them, and I knew that if I made one false step, I could pull them down with me into a life without hope.

My stepfather encouraged me to go to court and fight the mortgage company. So I went to the first court hearing and tried to explain to the judge how we'd come to be in the situation we were in. I told her how I'd signed away my legal right to live with my children in the home we'd worked so hard to own because my partner, under duress himself, had threatened me. I didn't know any of the legal words the mortgage company's lawyers used, and although I'd done research and learned as much as I could about the legal process involved, I didn't really understand it.

Thankfully, though, the judge believed what I said in court that day. She ordered the repossession process to be halted and told me, 'It is very important that you find a solicitor to represent you. You have what's called an "undue influence case", which means that it is not a foregone conclusion that the mortgage company will be able to repossess your house. Do you understand what I'm telling you? You *must* come to the next hearing with a solicitor.'

Although I'd been determined to fight the repossession order, I'd struggled to believe that I might have a chance of succeeding. So just the fact that the judge had listened to me and taken what I said seriously seemed like a major triumph.

I found a really good solicitor, and for the next two years he came with me to dozens of court hearings. At each hearing, the judge denied the mortgage company's request to start repossession proceedings, and the company's lawyers became more frustrated and bemused by the fact that I refused to back down. At one point, my solicitor told the mortgage company he was considering telling my story to the newspapers. 'They'll love it,' he said. 'I can just see the headlines: *Mortgage company supports domestic abuse. Hardworking mother of four young children is evicted from her home after her partner threatens her with physical violence and forces her to sign away her legal rights.*'

While the court case ground on, my solicitor managed to get a few thousand pounds knocked off some of our other debts, on the grounds, as the judge had explained to me, of 'undue influence'. But the mortgage company was proving more tenacious.

I didn't understand why they were so resolutely refusing even to consider what seemed to be a reasonable request. I wasn't asking them to cancel the mortgage and forgive the debt – all I was asking was that they reinstate it, so that I could start paying it myself. My solicitor was shocked by the fact that they'd allowed Ken to extend the mortgage way beyond what the house was actually worth. But I didn't really care about that. All I wanted was the opportunity to pay it so that the children and I could live in our house without the fear of being kicked out.

Finally, after a long and exhausting battle, which must have cost the mortgage company tens of thousands of pounds in legal fees, they agreed to reduce the amount of interest that had accrued and to allow me to pay an interest-only mortgage. I couldn't imagine how I was ever going to pay off the capital sum, but the important thing was that we could keep our home. I didn't care what I had to do to earn the money: my children were going to have a decent home in a good neighbourhood, and that was all that really mattered.

For the children's sake, I agreed to let Ken move back in to live with us, although I couldn't shake off the feeling that he'd let us down. We'd nearly lost everything, simply because he'd refused to go to the police when he needed help. But I was desperate not to break up our family, and so I stood by him.

Ironically, it wasn't until after I'd won the court case that I finally fell apart. I'd always refused to take anti-depressants, because doing so would have meant I was accepting the fact that I suffered from depression, just like my mother had always done. Now, though, I realised that

I'd been angry with Ken for refusing to accept the fact that he needed help, and I was doing the same. It felt like admitting that I'd failed; but there are some battles you simply can't fight all on your own, and I suppose the trick is to know which ones they are.

It took a while, but eventually the tablets the doctor gave me began to bring the world back into focus. They didn't make me happy – I accepted long ago that nothing will ever do that – but they did enable me to manage, and that's good enough.

MY BROTHER CHRIS has always been my best friend; he's the only person I can really relax with, because he shared my childhood and I know he loves me for who I really am. But although, as children, we'd often try to comfort each other and talk about the things that were happening to us, I haven't said very much in this book about how our childhood experiences affected Chris, because I don't feel that it's right to attempt to tell his story for him.

As a teenager, he'd become so wild and angry that sometimes the rage that swirled around inside him like boiling liquid would burst out of him and he'd attack someone. He was always good to me, but he was full of anger and resentment towards our mother and he'd often launch himself at her, shouting that he'd kill her, and I'd have to drag him off – as much for his sake as for hers.

When he graduated from glue sniffing to becoming heavily involved in taking drugs, he seemed to lose control of his life completely, and it got to the point when it was clear that either he was going to kill someone or someone was going to kill him.

Even when he was a sometimes-violent teenager, I loved him, as I'd always done, but I didn't know how to help him. It was the birth of my son that had been the trigger I needed to make me rethink what I was doing with my life. When Chris was young, though, there was nothing to prompt him to turn that corner – until something happened that brought him unexpectedly to a crossroads.

When he was 18, he lashed out in a rage at someone one day, injuring him quite badly, and he was sent to a detention centre. I was really afraid for him then, because I thought he'd just give up. He'd been brought up amongst criminals, drunks and drug addicts, and now that he was going to be incarcerated with more of the same type of people, I thought his fate had been sealed. Thankfully, though, it was a punishment that proved to be the making of him.

At the detention centre, he was taught a trade and he began to see in his head a different picture of the future he might be able to have. I went to visit him every two weeks, with my mother and my young son, and I could almost see the change in him from one visit to the next as the effects of the drugs wore off and his confidence gradually improved.

Shortly after Chris was released from the detention centre, he met a girl and fell in love, and she encouraged him to change his life and went with him when he was offered a job on the other side of the country.

With the support of his girlfriend, who later became his wife, the move finally enabled Chris to reinvent himself as the person he wanted to be. Like me, he felt driven by the need to escape from his childhood and to be better than everyone else. So he worked really hard and started going to night school, and each time he looked over his shoulder, his past seemed just a little bit further away. Before long, his hard work had paid off and he did so well in his job that he ended up as a director of the company he worked for.

Although we rarely saw each other after he moved away, I'd always kept in touch with Chris, and one day a couple of years ago he phoned me to say that he and his wife and children were moving back to live not far from us. Shortly afterwards, Chris and I set up a company together and although for me it meant starting again from scratch, as I had, quite literally, nothing after I returned from Spain, working with Chris felt like being given another chance.

Over the next few months, we put in a lot of hours of hard graft and, in the early days particularly, by the time the children had gone to bed at night, I'd often be too exhausted to walk up the stairs to my own bedroom. But it was worth it, because the company has gone from strength to strength and now employs several people, provides me with enough money to pay the mortgage on our house, and gives me the security I've craved all my life.

One of the reasons my brother and I work so well together is because we have common goals, born of our shared childhood experiences and fuelled by the same fear of being forced to return to having nothing. And I know that I can trust Chris.

We both still have difficulty trusting other people, so we employ members of our family, training them up and paying for them to go on courses and gain qualifications that will enable them to find other jobs and be successful should our own business ever fail. But we're determined to succeed. We don't ever again want to have to be afraid of being labelled 'worthless', and we want to show the uncle and aunt who were so good to us when we were children, who loved us and never judged us when we were teenagers, and who I used to wish were my parents, that they were right to have faith in us.

I haven't yet managed to pay off all our debts, but the business is growing and looks set to do really well next year – despite the current financial situation. For once, I've got something to look forward to, because I have complete faith in my brother and I know that, with him driving the company forward, we will succeed.

I'm 40 years old, and I've never talked to anyone about the abuse I suffered as a child. However much I try to rationalise it and to tell myself that children who are abused are not in any way to blame, I'm still ashamed about what happened to me. What Carl did to me damaged some part of me that will never recover. I know I'll never lose my deep-rooted sense of worthlessness, or the fear that threatens to engulf me whenever I think about what might lie ahead as I approach each new crossroads in my life.

The people who think they know me would probably say I'm a strong person who stays calm in a crisis and that I can be relied upon to sort out everyone else's problems. And it's true that I have to be in control. I've known what it's like to live with chaos, and I daren't loosen my grip and let it seep back into my life. I don't feel that I can trust anyone other than my brother and a few other members of my family, and I have no real friends, because I'm terrified that if someone starts to get close to me, they'll discover I'm not the person they think I am.

Sometimes though, I'm able to rationalise the way I feel about myself by thinking that if I knew a child and discovered they were being abused, it wouldn't change my opinion about them – other than to make my heart bleed for them. So I know that I should pity the child I used to be and that I shouldn't feel as though the events of my childhood have stigmatised me as an adult. But there are times when I can't help it.

In many ways, reviewing my life while writing this book has made me feel stronger. I'm living with my demons and, mostly, keeping them under control. I have a successful business, a good relationship with my brother and, despite everything, also with my mother. My mother still drinks, but her love for her grandchildren and husband, and their love for her, have been the incentives she needed finally to rein in the demons that ruled – and ruined – her life and so many others for so long. I'm still with Ken, and we're trying to rebuild our life together. But most importantly of all – and it's the one thing I'm really proud of – I have wonderful relationships with my children.

Every day I have to battle against the voice in my head that tells me to give up my struggle to survive. 'Why not commit suicide?' it asks me. 'What can you possibly have to live for?' And sometimes I almost give in – until I remember the terrible intensity of the fear I felt each time my mother tried to kill herself. My life as a child was miserable, and my mother was at least partly to blame for failing to protect me against all the unspeakable things that happened to me. But I loved her, despite everything, and my greatest fear when I was young was that one day she might succeed in taking her own life and leave me all alone in the world, without her.

My most cherished memory is of being a small child and lying curled up on my grandmother's knee with my head resting on the side of her armchair as she stroked my hair and sang 'Away in a Manger'. Whenever life gets too hard to bear, I think of that moment and wish I was back there again. I know, though, that I can't go back and rewrite my own childhood; I can't change all the terrible things that happened or erase the scars they left behind – both on my body and on my mind. But I know, too, that I have to do everything in my power to give each one of my children the childhood that every child deserves.

However difficult things become, I know that I can't take my own life, because all those years ago, when my eldest son was a baby, I made a promise to him that, whatever happened, I would always be there for him when he needed me. It's a promise I made again as each of my children was born, and it's a promise I'm proud to say I've kept.

One day, my children won't need me. But as long as they do, and as long as it's in my power to do so, I'll be here to protect them and to take care of them. Because that's what mothers are supposed to do.

Epilogue

I NEVER KNEW – or cared – where Carl had gone after he left our house almost 30 years ago. But while writing this book I heard he'd died. At first, I felt cheated. I suppose I'd hoped that one day he'd have to answer for what he did to me and for the indelible stain he left on my life. And then I remembered how my grandmother always used to say that God sees everything, and that it's His anger we need to fear when the Day of Judgement comes.

I hope she was right.